From Children to Champions!

Be a Winner—With God's Help Against All Odds

R.C. Self

WestBow
PRESS
A DIVISION OF THOMAS NELSON

Copyright © 2012 R.C. Self

All rights reserved. No part of this book may be used or reproduced by any means, graphic, electronic, or mechanical, including photocopying, recording, taping or by any information storage retrieval system without the written permission of the publisher except in the case of brief quotations embodied in critical articles and reviews.

WestBow Press books may be ordered through booksellers or by contacting:

WestBow Press
A Division of Thomas Nelson
1663 Liberty Drive
Bloomington, IN 47403
www.westbowpress.com
1-(866) 928-1240

Because of the dynamic nature of the Internet, any web addresses or links contained in this book may have changed since publication and may no longer be valid. The views expressed in this work are solely those of the author and do not necessarily reflect the views of the publisher, and the publisher hereby disclaims any responsibility for them.

Any people depicted in stock imagery provided by Thinkstock are models, and such images are being used for illustrative purposes only.

Certain stock imagery © Thinkstock.

ISBN: 978-1-4497-7067-9 (sc)
ISBN: 978-1-4497-7069-3 (hc)
ISBN: 978-1-4497-7068-6 (e)

Library of Congress Control Number: 2012922131

Printed in the United States of America

WestBow Press rev. date: 11/28/2012

To the children of New Mexico Christian Children's Home
To the children of
children's homes everywhere

To the champions who raise them!
To encourage every parent
with children in
residential homes,
adoptive homes, and
single-parent homes

To the
Christian Child and Family Services Association

"Keeping our eyes on Jesus, the champion …"
—Hebrews 12:2, NLT

A child and family adventure-land book about the children of the Bible and how, by God's grace, they became champions!

Contents

Acknowledgments xi
Introduction xiii
1. That's No Way To Raise a Kid! 1
2. Growing Up in Group Care 11
3. Favor and Favoritism 23
4. The Song of an Orphan 35
5. The Little Girl Who Ended a War 49
6. Running Away Naked 60
7. A Way-Out Teenager 71
8. Goliath Faces the Giant 80
9. The Prodigal Father 92
10. "Tell 'Em Who Your Daddy Is!" 102
11. Life after Juvey 113
12. A Lot of Bull and a Baby 126
13. Chances with the Champion 133
Endnotes 157
For more study 161

Acknowledgments

My wife, Liz, lived what I can only write about. She championed our children.

Without her support, this book would not have been written. Thanks, Honey, for your love.

My children taught me how to tell a story through many versions of chocolate chip bedtime Bible stories. Thanks to all five of you for enduring me.

My parents gave me a foundation of faith. I'm forever grateful.

Countless others have taught and encouraged me, supporting our organization and mission. Thank you for believing.

Introduction

In the land of Is Real,
  there were
    dinosaurs and dragons,
      earthquakes and floods,
        kings and queens,
          princes and princesses,
            wars and bloodshed.

The bad guys won some fights.
The good guys always won the battles.

Real losers were common.

The most exciting things about the land of Is Real were the superheroes.

They were children.

Doing what children do best, they sang!

Their songs were powerful and could not be stopped! Their chorus floated into the heavens covering the earth. The songs ended wars, defeated enemies, and destroyed all avengers![1]

The children achieved world peace!

They were called conquerors, victors, overcomers![2]

Led by a super Child sent down to earth from some other realm, they marched!

A planet changed. All birthdays centered round His.

Some grown-ups found His birthdate printed on their certificate. They were unhappy. They protested.
But no matter what they did, and even when they could not see Him, He was always there.

They said, "Oh, He's not real. He's imaginary."
But then they looked at their own certificates.

And there He was.

In the land of Is Real,
    the children were
        orphaned and abandoned,
            abused and mistreated,
                sneaking out at night and
                    scheming by day.

They were smart. But they did not always obey their parents.

So Someone Else had to take up the slack for them.

In the land of Is Real
    kids were adopted
        placed in group homes
            and foster care,
                and raised in single-parent homes.

Some were raised in two-parent homes with a good mother and father.

But all the kids had trouble—every one of them!
Even the super Child!

The land of Is Real is amazing. It's in the Bible, the book we call the Word of God. It's also where you and I live.

In the land of Is Real, the children grow up to become … champions!

This book is written to encourage faith. It's a call to strength! Every parent needs it. Every child must have it. What we believe makes all the difference between victory and defeat.

Parenting is the most challenging and important trip a person can take and growing up has never been more difficult.

We all want our children to be winners. So does God!

It's part of His game plan. But it's not a game. It's real life.

God holds the secrets to the universe. He made it.
So we follow His master plan.

In the land of Is Real,
    there were
    spirits and ghosts,
        invisible forces,
            demons and angels,
                witches and smoldering pots.

There were
    meanness and violence;
        a six-fingered, six-toed Gath;
        and a giant.

The enemy was led by the evil one.

There was God, and thousands of lesser gods.

But like the super Child, all the children grew up strong.

Like all the children of the Bible, and like ours,
their lives were an adventure …

    in the land of Is Real.

Chapter 1

That's No Way To Raise a Kid!

Before they were married, the worst possible thing happened.

Joe's girlfriend got pregnant. The baby didn't belong to him. He wasn't the father. The couple faced hard questions.

Everyone knew; that's no way to start a family.

Joe was devastated. He decided to break off the engagement and go quietly on his way.[3]

No Deadbeat Dad

The story is far too common.

You've heard it over and over. Unplanned pregnancies are tough. The girl gets pregnant, and the boy says, "I'm outta here! I'm not responsible. She's a big girl. She can answer for herself."

"I loved you that night, but this morning, catch me if you can! I'm moving to Tennessee or maybe Florida."

No forwarding address. No child support.

"You'll have to prove the baby is mine."

"No, I only met that girl once. Let's see, what was her name?"

The girl would be another one of the millions of single moms with the impossible task of being a full-time mother and a part-time father, doubling her career with the hard work of being a homemaker. Some societies don't allow for these social problems. They didn't in the land of Is Real. They stoned the guilty parties.

But Joe wouldn't walk away. He had planned a life of integrity.

He had simply fallen in love with someone who was thought to be a virtuous woman. When he proposed to her, she was a virgin. Obviously, he didn't know her as well as he thought. Still, it was better to find out now than to get married and end up in divorce. In the eyes of men, he had no legal obligation to the girl. He could walk away from her with a clear conscience.

But not with a clear heart.

Dreams do not die that easily. Love sometimes hurts.

Joe pondered over the pieces of a puzzle that didn't fit. But he was no deadbeat dad.

Pregnant Promises

The wedding vows had already been spoken.

Long before any public ceremony, they had embraced each other in arms of love. They pledged their commitment to God and each other, forever. They'd be together to their dying day. They vowed before God to make love last.

Binding marriage vows are often spoken, not at the wedding, but at engagement. Public vows take care of legal obligations. Private vows are deeper, tending to the obligations of love. True hearts are hard to find.

Too often, even private vows amount to nothing more than, "Honey, after another round of drinks, I'm going down on one knee to ask you a serious question."

But Joe wasn't like that! Where was his blessing? Why had God not honored his prayers? Did it mean nothing that he had pledged to be a real man?

He had promised not to run from responsibility, to be true to her through thick and thin, to treat her well from that day forward! He'd been taught to keep his word, no matter the cost.

Now she was pregnant!

Was he now excused from his promises to God? Was he released from his promises to the girl?

Desperate Decision

It blew Joe's mind that she still wanted to marry him.

Her feelings for him had not changed. She said that she wanted him now more than ever. Without him, she would be an outcast, shunned by her people, shamed by her religion. She desperately needed him.

True love speaks to the heart.

Although he didn't understand God or the girl or why his plans had taken an unplanned direction, his decision was to defend and protect her. Joe decided to move forward in faith.

He would marry the girl.

But he thought that it was certainly no way to start a family.

Born in a Barn

Times were hard.

The timing of this "surprise" was worse. The government required the new couple to travel to Bethlehem. No nice car with a heater. No stereo and reclining bucket seats. No motel stops along the way.

Somehow, they made it. He walked. She rode on the back of a donkey. They barely arrived in time for the baby to be born. No room at the inn. No extra cash. No doctor available.

Jesus was born in a barn, among animals. His first bed was a barn-box, a feeding trough. Surely a complaint was filed.

That's no way for a baby to be born.

Weird World

Eight days later, the baby was circumcised according to their custom.

It made absolutely no sense to most of the world. Why perform surgery on a perfectly healthy baby? Most people saw it as mutilation, some weird religious ritual.

"That's no way to treat a baby!"

Before they could even take the child home, word had spread of a paranoid, crazy, old, demented king, who had ordered that all the baby boys be killed.

There was no time to pack. They fled to Egypt. The couple narrowly escaped. They saved the baby's life.

But that was no time or place to raise a kid.

Mom's Mess

The mother of Jesus was very young when he was born. Mary was only a teenager.

Did she hesitate when the nurse or the priest gave her the birth certificate to sign? When she came to the dotted line where it named the father, what did she write? Just identifying the father's name was a real dilemma for an honest mother.

Legally, what would Jesus call Joe?

Stepdad? Kind of, but not really.

Foster dad? Yes, in a way, but it didn't totally fit.

An adoptive dad? Well, maybe.

How could Mary explain the whole story to the authorities? There would be an investigation to see whether the government should take the case. There would be a home study and reams of paperwork. Counseling would be recommended.

No, all things considered, it was much easier to simply identify the father as Joe.

But everyone knew, "That's no way to start a kid out with a dad!"

And what about Mom? Mary's reputation around town was ruined. Even those closest to her did not believe her story. If she was pure, she sure did not feel it from those who loved her most. They questioned her. They doubted. Even after she finally convinced Joseph to agree to marry her, people were whispering.

She certainly had not planned her pregnancy.

That's the family where Jesus entered the picture on planet Earth.

Doubly Difficult

Jesus wasn't raised by his biological father.

But Jesus accepted Joseph as his dad. The neighborhood recognized Jesus as the "son of the carpenter."[4] Jesus referred to himself as the "Son of Man." Still, their relationship was different from any other.

The family was different from any other, too. Jesus had at least six younger brothers and sisters. Joe knew, without a doubt, that they were his kids. They belonged to him.

But not that other one!

If Joe was normal at all, he had days when he had a hard time accepting Jesus as his son. He must have questioned himself at times. Had an angel really spoken to him in a dream? Could he really believe Mary's side of the story?

Who was this kid who he was teaching to swing a hammer? Who was this kid who claimed to be his firstborn? Were the parents open about his adoption, or did they keep it a secret? Did they tell him early and often that he wasn't really Joseph's, or did they wait until he was older?

Did Jesus ever have a jealous thought as he saw Joseph care for his younger siblings? Was he ever tempted to say, as so many do in blended families, "Back off, you're not my dad!"

Parenting is one of the most difficult jobs. Step-parenting can be doubly hard.

Fatherless Family

As everyone predicted, this dysfunctional family had their share of trouble. But twelve years later, somehow they were still together.

That's No Way To Raise a Kid!

During a family vacation of sorts, they journeyed in a huge caravan to Jerusalem. Days later, when it came time to get ready to leave for home, the parents lost track of their oldest boy in all the commotion. Mom thought that Dad was in charge of him. Dad thought that Mom knew where he was. They both thought that he was among friends and relatives of the caravan. They weren't worried, until later, after a full day of traveling toward home, when they didn't find the boy in any of the wagons.

Of course, Dad is responsible for all this! He's the head of the family.

Just about the time that he thinks the oldest boy in the family can take care of himself, just when Joe is hoping to get a break, a little breather, just when he thinks that he only needs to take care of the little ones, Jesus gets lost.

Joe has to leave the caravan and spend a whole day traveling back to Jerusalem to search for his lost "dream kid." Three days later, Joe finally locates him. Another complaint was filed.

You would think that Jesus would apologize to Joe. Instead, he just said, "I have to be about my father's business."

It's the last we ever hear of Joe—tracking down his lost child in the big city. No one knows what happened to Joe afterward. Maybe he was accused of abuse or neglect. Poverty may have sent him straight to jail.

Joe was likely told many times by the authorities, "That's no way to raise a kid."

Maybe it was all just too much for him to take. Maybe he died from a heart attack or stress-related illness. We don't know whether Joe abandoned the family. We will never know for sure if he separated from Mary. After all, he had threatened divorce before.

Whatever the reason, it appears that Mary struggled along alone, raising Jesus and his younger brothers and sisters without a father in a single-parent home.[5]

Single Savior

Jesus grew up fast.

He took over the carpenter shop at an early age. Early on, he tried to be the man of the family.

And what did Jesus grow up to be?

A carpenter? That was His occupation.

A preacher? He did that, too, but it didn't pay well.

A world-changer? Yes, that, too. Those are all great things He did. But what did He grow up to be?

He grew up to be … single.

Single!

Does that sound anti-climactic? "Is that all?" you object. Jesus was the son of God!

Do you seriously mean to simply say He ended up single? What's the point?

The point is, we can all relate. If you're single, you find your greatest encouragement right here. After years in your own family! After all your childhood dreams! After years of education! After starting your own career! Perhaps you were happily married; perhaps not. Perhaps you were married once, twice, or three times, or perhaps not at all.

In the end, you're going to be single; solo before God.

Jesus was. That's how He ended up. In many ways, He lived a simple life. He chose to be single.

There were probably days He thought about dating Martha. Singles have days they want to be married, and married folks have days they wish they were single.

What Jesus grew up to be helped Him do what He did. He used being single to His advantage. He was single so He could be part of a greater family. He was single to find a deeper love. He developed intimate relationships. He considered everyone family.

Oh, yes, He had lots of friends. He had more family than most ... because He was single. And being single kept Him in a close walk with God.[6]

There are times when being single is not easy. On the cross, Jesus never felt more alone. He cried out, "My God! My God! Why have you forsaken me?" In his humanity and final moments of despair, He questioned, "This is how I end up? Is this all I'll ever amount to? Single? Alone?"

For the average person, that would be the end. But Jesus believed there was a resurrection. Victory was just ahead. He had only to endure to the end.

On the cross, Jesus was declared champion![7]

He became our Savior.

Christian Champions

Our country has grown keenly aware of the victories of singles.

Half of the families in the United States are classified as single-parent homes. They make important contributions to our country. We celebrate Presidents who were raised in single-parent homes. Single parents and their children are valuable, useful, and needed.

Jesus gave His life on the cross to make every single person a champion. He became like us in every way, facing all the adversity and suffering we have faced and more. His purpose was to show that all children can live victoriously. He gives us the grace we need to be like Him: champions![8]

God's best plan for a family is for every child to have a mother and a father. That's where children find the greatest blessings. When there's no father around, we must equip mothers to go forward in strength. When there's no mother around, we must encourage fathers to raise their kids to be Christian champions.

Expecting the Exceptional

Jesus wasn't raised in a normal family.

He wasn't raised to be normal. He was exceptional. Beginning in lowly circumstances, high expectations were placed on him. Adversities, difficulties and struggles are the very things that qualified him to be our champion.

That gives us hope. We can relate.

We all have some unique family history that's different from anyone else's. There's that crazy grandmother or uncle, not to mention our own parents. They are all characters.

The odds were against Jesus, too. His family life had the greatest difficulties to overcome:

>premarital, unplanned pregnancy,
>step-parent and adoptive issues,
>single-parent problems.

"That's no way to raise a kid!"

They said it about Jesus. They said it to his parents. They will say it about you or any exceptional champion-to-be.

It's to be expected…

in the land of Is Real.

Chapter 2

Growing Up in Group Care

She loved her only son more than anything. Her love was deep and strong, pure and unselfish.

But you would question her love.

Her son was only three years old, barely weaned off her breast, when she placed him in residential care in a children's home.

She was simply doing what she thought was best for her boy. She wanted him to have the best life possible. She could not give it to him. Hannah's life had been full of turmoil and misery for too many years.

Crazy Circumstances

Her husband loved her. At least he said he did.

During their marriage, however, he fathered children with another woman. This other woman was a great source of grief for her. When her husband expressed pride in those kids, it caused her pain. Before her son was born, the situation nearly drove her insane.

But she wouldn't leave her husband. She was faithful to him. And like so many girls, she thought that giving him a son would help their relationship.

For years she tried to get pregnant, but she wasn't able. Being childless, she hurt. Friends around town never knew how deeply. She wept over their thoughtless comments.

Hannah was an outcast, excluded from the local social networks. Conversation with other women was strained. She didn't participate in parent-teacher meetings or Little League soccer. Her self-confidence was gone. She was empty.

There was only one thing she could think of that would change her world. She wanted her own child more than anything. Just one!

So she prayed.

She prayed not because she was such a great believer in God. These were not particularly religious times and territories. She prayed because she did not know what else to do. She prayed out of desperation.

Professional people misunderstood her. They assumed her problem was substance abuse—perhaps alcohol or drugs. Mental illness was a possibility.

She didn't eat right. Her weeping was uncontrollable. She appeared to talk to herself. She appeared to be—well, let's just say it—crazy!

Even in her depression, Hannah was never completely defeated. She never stopped praying at home or in public. Prayer was her only friend. Prayer was where she could dream.

But it didn't seem to be working. God didn't promise her a child. After years of prayer, she took her prayers to the next level, a deeper level that you might question.

She bargained with God.

From Depression to Dreams

Hannah had nothing to offer, yet she promised to give God something she didn't have.

It was a promise she intended to keep.

"O, Lord, Almighty, if You will give me a son, I'll give him right back to you all the days of his life."[9]

It was a promise for a promise.

If God showed His favor, her great personal crisis would end. She would give her greatest dream, her only son, over to God. If she had a son, she would not cling to him. She would not hold him back in any way. She would free him to be God's boy. No longer would people treat her as second-class. For once she would know that her life was, after all, a plan of God.

Finally, in promising her own life-dream to God, she found peace. When she made that promise, she began eating right. She put on a happy face. The anguish and grief was gone. The depression left. She just gave up and believed.

All this, before God even answered her prayer.

Happy Houseful

"In the course of time, Hannah conceived and gave birth to a son. She named him Samuel, which means, 'Ask the Lord.'"[10]

When Sammy was born, it was a happy-Hannah day. God had kept His promise first.

Three years later, Hannah did not back out on her promise.

"After he was weaned, she took the boy with her, young as he was ... and brought him to live in Shiloh, in the House of the Lord, where he worshipped."[11]

Imagine that: a three-year-old who worships the Lord. Never underestimate the importance of teaching kids at an early age. Toddlers who learn to sing and pray are happier in the long run. Children who enter the House of God will be blessed.

Hannah let Sammy grow up in the Shiloh Children's Home. She never looked back on her decision in doubt. She never faulted herself. She did not sink back into depression. She continued to trust her life to God.

She loved Sammy, visited when she could, and brought him chocolate-chip cookies.

Hannah was so happy after she released Samuel into God's care at Shiloh. "You make me strong and happy, Lord," she prayed. "You rescued me. Now I can be glad and laugh at my enemies."

On and on she gave praise.[12]

Far beyond her dreams, she went on to bear five more children! That means God not only answered her prayer but saw she was better suited to take on children as a believer than she had been before. Her blessings were multiplied when she believed.

Without help, Hannah may not have been able to provide the best life for Sammy. But that did not make her a loser. It wasn't the story of her whole life. God was not unhappy with her. She fit right into His plan.

She went on to be a Godly mother of a houseful of her own kids.

Giving to God

Here's a truth we can't get around.

All parents must give their children back to God, and the sooner the better! The sooner parents dedicate their children to God, the greater the blessing. When parents decide to raise their children by the plans of God, they move them ahead of the class. Kids who attend Sunday school are better prepared to start kindergarten than kids who don't. The blessings are many.

Growing up in Shiloh Children's Home wasn't easy for Sammy. After all, growing up is tough for the best of kids in the best of situations.

On paper, Sammy's family background wasn't the best. The strikes were against him. But his experience eventually trained him for God's purpose better than anyone could.

The road his mother put him on led him to become God's boy, the greatest of all prophets.

Inside, Not Outside

Sammy's "house parent" was Eli, the priest.

By our standards, he was not qualified to raise God's boy. He was too old to raise a little one.

He had tremendous trouble raising his own two sons. They were two bad examples for Sammy to grow up around.

Still, God used Eli to raise the child into a great champion!

Even in this situation, "the boy Samuel was busy serving ... and growing up in the presence of the Lord."[13]

Do you serve in a place far from perfect? God's presence is there to help you get through!

Are you growing up in a situation that is less than the best? God will help you overcome and grow from God's boy into God's man, from God's girl into God's woman.

Simply growing up in a Christian home does not make one a Christian. At the same time, being raised with unique family handicaps does not make you a loser. God looks into the heart.

What grows inside a person, in a person's heart, is greater than anything on the outside.[14]

Ending Up ... Down

Eli's sons were immoral, mean thieves.

They mocked religious training while serving at the altar of God. The Lord saw their hypocrisy, and it made Him sick.[15]

Sammy saw it, too. He witnessed as Eli rebuked his sons and tried to correct them. The boys would not listen. They did not care about their own father, even though they lived with him.

If you're a child who lives with your mother and father, be thankful. Listen to their instruction. Many children do not have your privilege and blessing.

But if you are like Sammy and do not live with your parents, God still has His greatest blessing planned for you. Be sure of it.

The most important factor is not whether you live with your mother and father. What really counts is living in God's presence, listening to His instruction. Children get the favor and blessing of Almighty God through obedience to His Word. It's a Biblical law and promise.

If you disobey God's Word, you will end up... down.

No-Fret Faith

Sammy knew what his mother told him. God was taking care of him through Eli, the priest.

Eli provided for him the best he could, but Eli wasn't Sammy's real father.

His biological father, Elkanah, was not doing anything to raise Sammy.

Sammy loved both Eli and Elkanah, but from the beginning, Sammy knew what his mother had told him: His life was planned out by his true father, his Heavenly Father.

And God's plan is always for our good.

Today, many parents are in Eli's situation. They see their grown kids going down the wrong path. They think, "We should have done this or that, moved here or there. We should have protected them more." They fret with regret.

Parents should not do that. They should never re-walk a path to the past. They should not say, "We have been led to the middle of nowhere. All this time, God was not with us."

It's not true. God is always with us.

Parents are responsible for teaching their kids and setting the right example, and when God's boy becomes a man, he's responsible. He's accountable for his own actions.

Parents must be encouraged to put regrets away. Endless grieving does no good. Don't live in discouragement! That's what the evil one, the destroyer, the accuser, wants you to do.

Turn your discouragement into victory by faith. Do it today! As long as God is in the picture, victory is still in sight. There is always one thing you can do, and it is absolutely the best. It's what Hannah did.

No matter how good or bad your situation is, always ask the Lord.

You can always pray for your children.

It's powerful when you kindly—with no strings attached—let your kids know that you dream the best for them in prayer.

Boys to Bills to Men

When Eli's boys were grown men, he could not stop their misbehavior. He tried, but it was a hard place for a parent to be.

As children get older, they need more space. It's God's natural will that children eventually leave their parents. That was one of Eli's mistakes. Unlike Hannah, he hung on to his kids. While he appeared to help his sons and kept them in ministry, he was actually holding them back. He prevented them from ever growing up.

His sons should have graduated from the Shiloh Children's Home and moved on. Instead, living off the sacrifices of others, they abused their privileges and let other people pay.

There is only one thing that cures eighteen-itis: Kindly let grown children pay their own bills!

Finding Favor

Eli couldn't beat his sons, so he joined them.

He should have never eaten the food his sons stole from the people when they made sacrifices at the altar of God.[16] With this stolen food, Eli became seriously overweight.

Unconditional love never participates in wickedness. It would have been better to eat Corn Flakes. When he gave in to his boys, he lost what little respect they had for him instead of finding their favor.

Sammy grew up in the middle of all of this. He still turned out to be God's boy. Circumstances do not make one successful in God's eyes.

These kids were all raised in the same House of the Lord, in the same church. Eli's boys were despised and hated. Samuel became the great prophet of God.

Hannah's story wasn't so bad after all. Her seed of faith, her teaching planted in the heart and mind of Samuel, was powerful. Her faith grew inside him throughout his lifetime. She asked the Lord for help, and Sammy learned to do the same.

Sammy just kept on believing what his mother told him, that it was God's plan for him to grow up in Shiloh. With this faith, "The boy Samuel continued to grow tall and strong, in favor with the Lord and men."[17]

Words of Warning

One day, a preacher came to Shiloh.

He was delivering to Eli, the priest, a word from the Lord. The word had not been getting through to many people in those days, not in the land of Is Real, not as long as Eli and his sons were in charge of Shiloh.

The Lord said, "I will honor only those who honor me. But those who despise me, I will despise."

That sounds like a familiar principle, like a promise for a promise. The words predicted Eli's end. They warned Eli that his sons' lives would be cut short, but if they listened, there would be time to make a change.

A warning is a chance to consider another way. A warning is a sign of God's patience. A warning is another chance to become a champion.

Hard of Hearing

Years later, Samuel was still only a boy serving the Lord in the Shiloh Children's Home.

Eli was now very heavy, very old, and almost blind. Add hard-of-hearing to his list of problems. The word of the Lord had not gotten through to Eli for years, so God finally gave up trying to get Eli to listen. Instead, He called one night to Samuel. He called him by name.

Sammy got up, went to Eli, and said, "I'm here!"

Eli said, "I did not call you. Go back to your bed and lie down."

Again, the Lord called, "Samuel!"

Samuel went to Eli, and asked, "You called me?"

Eli said, "No, I did not. Go back to bed."

When the Lord called the third time, Eli realized that He must be speaking to him. "Stay in your room, Samuel," Eli told him. "Ask the Lord."

Parents often use the first line. There are better reasons to use the second.

The word of the Lord was now getting through directly to Samuel in his night-time prayers. These were words the people would need to hear in order to be blessed.

Good News, Bad News

The Lord let Samuel know He was not on speaking terms with Eli.

Eli's position as priest, his age as an elder, his title, money, and power–none of that mattered. The Lord was now on speaking terms with a young boy whose heart was open and full of faith.

That night, Sammy learned that Eli and his sons would soon be removed from service. Their lives would end up ... down.

The Lord instructed Samuel to continue serving, hearing, and speaking in God's house. Samuel was to become the leader of God's people in the land of Is Real.

The next morning, Eli insisted that Samuel tell him what the Lord said in the night. When he heard the message, even Eli knew that what was bad news for himself and his two sons was good news for Samuel and the people.

Eli said, "He is Lord. Let Him do what is good in His eyes."[18]

Christian Champion

Eli's bully sons were a couple of clever cowards.

Clever enough to avoid the military draft, they protected themselves from war by pretending to serve in the House of God. However, during their time of leadership, God was put aside and Is Real lost its way. God no longer protected a nation that had become so wicked. Four thousand soldiers were killed in battle with the Philistines.

The people of the land of Is Real gathered together and scratched their heads.

"Why," the elders asked, "are the people of God being defeated in battle? When God is on our side, we are never defeated!"

"Let us now bring the ark of God from Shiloh to lead us into battle, and let's make those two priestly sons of Eli carry it to the front line. After all, they are men of God. They have God's protection if anyone does."

When this was done, the slaughter was great. Thirty thousand foot soldiers were killed in the land of Is Real. The ark of God was captured, and Eli's sons were killed.

A runner was commissioned to go to Shiloh to give Eli the news. When Eli heard it, he fell over in his chair and died. This event marked a new beginning in the land of Is Real, the beginning of Samuel's leadership.

He became the greatest prophet of his day. He returned the people and the ark to the Lord. As long as Samuel was in leadership, they were never defeated by the Philistines.

God's boy had become God's man, raised up to lead the people back to God, raised up to become a champion of the Lord.

Samuel means, "Ask the Lord"!

Every parent who wants to raise a Christian champion must do just that.

Chapter 3

Favor and Favoritism

In the land of Is Real, long before ultrasound or fertility drugs, before test strips and sonograms, she knew she was pregnant.

And something was wrong. There was something weird going on in her womb! But then, isn't any womb strange in its own way?

Every day she examined her stomach. It was out of control, growing way too fast. It pulled over to one side, and then leaned to the other. A bump here. A lump there.

It was a bumpalumpus!

Pushing and Shoving

She cried out to the Lord, "What in the world is happening to me?"

Nine months was an eternity to wait to find out.

Twin babies jostled within Rebekah.[19] Her womb was a ring for some big-time wrestling.

After months of feet to the ribs and elbows in the eyes, the first baby boy pushed his way through the birth canal. He was named Red because of his hair. The second boy, Jake, was born right on the heels of the first.

The first boy was so wanted. The second was a surprise, more than the parents asked for. Honestly, a lot more.

Even after they were born, the boys continued to wrestle, and Red usually won. About the only time Jake won was when he caught Red off guard. You know how it is: he could beat his brother when he back-jumped him!

Principled Parents

From the time the boys were young, their parents believed it was good to keep them separated, so Dad took one while Mom handled the other.

Jake would have done anything to be his father's favorite.

Like normal kids, the boys competed for their parents' love and attention. They knew how to play their parents against each other.

Red, who was into everything, grew up fast. He spent lots of time with his father. Like his dad, he became a skillful hunter. They were always outdoors together. His dad instilled great confidence in him as his favorite boy. Red learned to believe in himself. There was nothing he could not do.

Jake, on the other hand, could not compete on Red's turf and terms, so he learned a different way to win. Quietly, strategically, he helped with the household chores and became handy in the kitchen. He found his mother's favor by staying home.

Growing up, watching his parents play favorites, Red adopted the same principles he saw in his parents. He practiced what he learned from them. He didn't need everyone, just his favorites.

He decided, for example, that he could do quite well without his mother. It was only a small step from there to having the same attitude toward his father. Eventually, he didn't need anyone. He became overly independent. In other words, Red became disconnected.

Red took his parents for granted. Today, we might call it an attachment disorder or maybe just teenage rebellion. Whatever it was, the feeling he once had for his parents was gone.

Independence is good to a point, but for all the good qualities independence offers, it's never good to say, "I don't need you, Mom. I don't need your love. I don't need a relationship with Dad anymore." That's going way too far.

While parents are raising strong, independent children, love never says, "You're on your own, so don't ever call again."

No, real love relationships last a lifetime. Inter-dependence is a healthy concept.

A family depends on each other.

Gut Feelings

Red began going on hunting trips without his father.

His dad was so proud, but in the back of his mind, like most parents, he worried. Something didn't seem right.

Parents must be careful when it looks like their kids are growing up too fast. In so doing, parents may lead their own kids into temptation, all in the name of love and provision. It's important our kids don't get independent too early in life.

Favor and favoritism grow together in the pit of the stomach. Sometimes parents see them for what they are, but only after they've been given birth.

Red began hanging around with the wrong crowd. The trips away from home grew longer, and he brought home a different kind of wild game: girls. He dated girls who drove his mother nuts.

These girls did not believe in God, but Red didn't care. Moral and religious beliefs were his parents' problem. If they didn't like it, he would just leave. In fact, Jake had actually heard Red say he despised his family heritage.

If his parents heard that, it would hit them where it hurts!

Eyes to See

One day, Red came home from hunting.

Hungry, he went to the kitchen, where Jake was stirring a fresh pot of his favorite "Red" stew.

Red said, "Quick, give me some of that."

Jake said, "It'll cost you."

"How much?"

"Not much—just something you've bragged that means nothing to you, something you don't need or care about, something you said you could do without. You said you despised your birthright."

If Jake thought Red was going to back down, he was wrong. Red wasn't going to swallow his pride. He was not about to eat his own words for supper. He wanted something to satisfy the growling from his hunger pangs, the wrestling he felt in his stomach.

"You can have it!" answered the redhead, and he sold his birthright for a pot of stew.

He took off a special armored bracelet his father had made for him and tossed it to Jake.

But the father knew none of this. Isaac was old and had grown completely blind. Like so many parents whose eyes are wide open, he couldn't see what was going on in his own house.

Birthright and Blessing

One day, Isaac told Red to go hunting for him one last time.

He said, "I want you bring home some wild game and prepare me a special meal. Cook it my favorite way, like your mother does. I have something special to give you before I get any older, before I start getting sick and then die."

He intended to bless Red by declaring him the future head of the family.

Rebekah knew what was going on and did not like it one bit. While Red was out hunting, she brought Jake in and told him she was going to trick the old, blind Isaac into giving Jake his formal blessing. She put goat skins and hair on Jake's smooth arms so they would feel like Red's. Then she cooked a meal for Isaac with all his favorite spices and sent Jake in to take the food trays to his father.

Jake objected to all this at first.

He said, "Mother, what if Dad discovers me and calls down a curse on me instead of a blessing?"

She said, "Let the curse fall on me instead. Now do as I say."

Pretending to be Red, Jake delivered the food to his father. When Jake spoke, Isaac said, "You sound like Jake."

Jake said, "No, it's me, Esau!"

"Come here," Isaac said. He smelled the usual animal odor on his clothes, felt the hairy arms and hands, and felt the birthright, the home-made armored band that Isaac had given him.

Finally convinced, Isaac pronounced the irrevocable family blessing on Jake. He took a matching family arm brace from his own forearm and placed it on Jake's other arm.

Responsibility and Respect

Soon after Jake left the room, Red came in with a prepared meal.

Isaac then realized that Jake had tricked him.

Red was more than irate. He said, "First, he tricked me out of my birthright. Now, he tricks you out of my family blessing."

Red was so angry he threatened to kill Jake. If he could get him in one more wrestling match, he'd break his neck.

Red is an example of so many teenagers. They can do just fine without their parents. They don't need help from teachers or advice from authority figures. They can make it on their own.

Then, when faced with paying their own bills, they understand things in a different light. They see what they took for granted after it's gone.

Those great twin character-builders, responsibility and respect, are the real family birthrights and blessings.

Jacob at the Jabbok

It was a divided house.

Jake was now fully grown, and favoritism had split his family in two.

Jake left home with the words of his brother echoing in his mind, "If you ever come back, I'll kill you."

Twenty years later, Jacob is at the Jabbok River.

Perspiration beaded his forehead as he camped at the border. Just across the Jabbok River was his homeland, the land of Is Real, the land his father promised to give him. He didn't know whether he should cross back over that line. There'd be no band playing at his homecoming. If he went into Red's territory, it was the drumbeat of war that worried him.

It was now or never. After twenty years, he had to face his brother.

He planned to pacify Red with a lifetime of accumulated treasure. After all, he had more than enough to spare. God had favored him and blessed him far beyond his dreams.

Restitution might ease their reunion. He sent 580 head of livestock ahead as a gift to make peace. He prayed it would work but worried it would be taken as a bribe or insult.

Here, twenty years later, Jacob was still wrestling and being pinned by his brother.

He sent his family, sons, servants, and all his possessions across the Jabbok.

It's almost as if he were trying to talk himself into following.

Wrestling and Winning

Jacob sat there in No Man's Land.

Everyone and everything he loved was now on the other side. Fear and faith wrestled within. Night surrounded him. All alone, he prayed.

"God save me. I'm terrified."

Then, the Bible says, out of the darkness, out of the bushes, out of nowhere, a man back-jumped him, and Jacob wrestled him until daybreak.[20]

This was big-time wrestling. Headlocks and full Nelsons! Hammer holds and leg locks! All night long they flopped over the rocks and flipped into the Jabbok.

Since Esau was on his mind, Jake wondered if it could possibly be his brother.

What happened next sounds strange. "When the man saw that he could not overpower Jake, he touched his hip, so that it was wrenched out of socket."[21]

He could not overpower Jake, but all it took was a "touch" to wrench his hip socket. It only took a "touch" to bruise the largest, most powerful bone in Jake's body.

Who was this man? Whose face was hidden by darkness of night?

The man said, "Your name will no longer be Jacob (Man Cheater), but Israel (God Wrestler) because you have struggled with God and with men and have overcome."[22]

Jacob was declared the winner!

New Name

Who wins when we wrestle God?

That's easy, you say. God wins. He knows everything. He's all powerful. He's everywhere at once. You can't whip almighty God!

Can you?

Like a father and son in a marquee match on the living room floor, we wrestle.

The father says, "You're wearing me out! I give! You're champion!"

The toddler dances around the room. He raises his arms in victory. He beats his chest and says, "Yeah, I win! I beat Dad!" The celebration goes on and on. The toddler never lets the father forget.

Isn't that what our Heavenly Father did for us through Jesus?

Jesus took the form of a man. He went to the cross. He died to let us live.

We see him hanging there. Nailed. Out of breath. Bleeding. Pinned for the count.

He says, "I lose. You win."

He doesn't overpower us. He just wants to touch us.

And on the cross, He does. He touches our hearts with his love.

Like Jacob, we may not be the fastest or the strongest. Even after we've wrestled with God, we continue to limp along in life, still hampered by human failings. But none of that matters. For the rest of our days, we are given a new identity. We have a new name.

Gladiator! Champion! Christian!

Never again a loser!

Struggling to Succeed

God wants us to be winners.

He will see to it that we are victors.

The blessings of wrestling with Him far outweigh the suffering.

Wrestling God involves a struggle. It takes everything we have to win. We wrestle as if our very lives depend on it. It involves pain and exhaustion.

We almost give up, but the Heavenly Father is incapable of hurting the son.

He takes us right up to our limit.

He knows when we've had just enough to make us grow. It is not easy, but the end results in blessing and success.

Right Relationships

Jake asked the man his name.

The man answered, "Why do you ask?"

Then, mysteriously, the man was gone. Jake then realized whom he had been wrestling and said, "I have seen God face-to-face."

When he crossed the Jabbok, Jake was limping. But it wasn't a loser's limp.

The sun came up as the disheveled Jake crossed over the Jabbok where his family camped. He looked over the land and saw the Red army dotting the hills.

One man stood out in front. From a distance, the two brothers stared at each other.

Jake went to his knees and bowed low to the ground. It was a signal of surrender.

Then Red led what appeared to be the charge.

But his army stayed behind. Red was not attacking. He was eagerly racing to meet Jake and embrace him. He threw his arms around his neck and kissed him, and they wept.

Red said, "What's the meaning of all the livestock you sent to me?"

Jake replied, "I want to find favor in your eyes. I want to be right with my brother. For to see your face is like seeing the face of God, now that you've received me favorably."

Jake explained that he had been favored beyond measure, just as his father foretold. But Red refused the generous gift, explaining that he, too, had been highly favored.

Both men looked back on twenty years of separation, realizing that God had blessed each of them. All their needs were met. They lacked nothing.

God's favor is unconditional and shows no favoritism.

God rejects no one.

When He blesses one, He does not exclude another.

Face to Face

Finally, Jake understood.

The face of his brother was superimposed upon the mystery man whose face he was not allowed to see.

He pondered the mysterious reply, "Why do you ask my name?"

No answer was given because, when we wrestle with God, his name may be Red or Esau. It may be Terry, Bill, or Charles. It may be Liz, Jula, or Janice.

Every day we see the face of God in those around us.

A brother's favor can be God's healing favor.

Unfair Favor

There are two philosophies of winning.

One is a deception that says, "Leave God out. Be a cheater. You can win if you steal, cheat, and lie. Put yourself first." But in the end, there is no lasting victory.

Here's a winning formula that really works: Include God in your life struggles. Wrestle with Him. Treat your fellow man well. Put others first. Show mercy and grace. You will find God's favor and man's.

Good parents know the difference between favor and favoritism.

Holding back love in the presence of siblings is not the answer. Every child is to be favored in his or her own unique way. Every child is to be consistently the favorite of both parents. That way, there's no favoritism.

If both boys are secure in their parents' love, it never hurts to say, "Red, I love you the most, with all my heart! Jake, you're the favorite of all my kids. I couldn't love you more."

Just make sure you say it to both of them at the right time. Let them both know your unlimited and unfailing love.

Why is that not wrong to say?

Because God says the same thing to every one of us!

"R.C., you are My son! You are so special to Me! If you were the only person left on earth, I would still send My other son, Jesus, to die for you!"[23]

Wow!

If I were on my brother Jesus' side of that statement, that would sound unfair, like favoritism—in my favor!

Chapter 4

The Song of an Orphan

A little orphan boy cried alone in his room. Even though he'd never known his mother, he missed her deeply.

She died giving birth to him, sacrificing her life for his.

That was the best news of his life. And it was all he knew about her.

So he missed her love.

No Green Grass

He was living in his second foster home.

The orphan boy didn't know what happened to his first foster mother. Too young to know, he thought perhaps she had abandoned him. So he was bitter toward her.

By all appearances, his second foster home was worse than the first.

He was taken to a small village out in the middle of nowhere; a dry, dusty, deserted, desert of a place. As far as the eye could see down the dark valley, everything was rocks and sand. The people of the village were all too familiar with dirt storms. There was no vegetation, nothing green.

The little bilingual town was so small that you wondered how it could qualify to have a post office. For those who lived there, including the boy, it was more of a hiding place than a town.

The town was named Lodebar, which means "no pasture, no green grass."

Dramatic Day

The orphan boy didn't see it.

How could this second foster home be better than the first?

It didn't matter. He had no choice. He had to give it a chance.

He felt as though he were nothing but a government paycheck to his first foster mom. He would never recover from her care, never. Because of her, he lost the ability to trust people, adults, those in power over his life.

But he was told it wasn't all her fault. In fact, it wasn't her fault at all that his life had taken its worst turn. It wasn't her fault his father was killed serving in military action.

His father was a great man, a war hero, strong and courageous. Stories of his adventures were legendary. But he remembered his father as the most loving and gentle man in the world, his daddy.

His life changed dramatically that day, when he was five years old. The news stormed into the quarters with screams and shrieks that his father had been killed. The enemy was upon them. The escape plan was simply every man for himself.

Cry of a Cripple

In the chaotic evacuation, his nurse jerked him up by one arm and took off running.

That hurt, but not as much as when she stumbled, dropped him, and fell on top of him. The pain was excruciating, but strangely he could feel nothing in his feet. Nothing!

In her panic, she fussed at him to stop crying and to get up and run.

He couldn't.

Frantically, she badgered him just to get up and walk. She didn't know how much he was hurt. He couldn't move his feet.

A servant running by heard the crying and stopped just long enough to pick him up and set him on a cart. He needed immediate medical attention, but all he got was a long, bumpy ride.

He never saw a doctor. Crying did no good, but he cried until he was exhausted and could cry no more.
He was paralyzed at the ankles.

A five-year-old shouldn't be a casualty of adult wars, but in the land of Is Real, children are usually the first to suffer as wounded in action.

He didn't know which was worse, losing his dad or losing his feet and becoming crippled for life.

Both felt equally bad.

Name Shame

The orphan boy lost more than his father and feet that day.

Two uncles and a grandfather were taken from him as well, all in the same battle. All four of them were on the side of good, but the bad guys won the fight.

He wanted to believe what his dad had taught him, but it didn't make sense. He wanted to believe that God would always care for him, that the Lord's very name was victory and victory was given to the Lord's champion.

It sure didn't look like it.

He remembered the best feeling of his life: when his dad told him he was his champion, his only champion.

But being a champion was scary now. His dad had given him a warrior's name; the name Merib-baal. The name meant anti-Baal, against Baal.

Baal was one of the world's great religions. Millions of people called Baal a powerful god. Among many things, they called him the lord of the land. But his dad told him Baal was nothing but a stone-cold, powerless idol.

His dad proudly said, "Merib-Baal, you will be a champion against Baal."

Now, before he was old enough to understand, his dad was dead, killed by the people of Baal.

His dad was none other than Jonathan, the prince, the oldest son of the King, next in line to be king.

Merib-Baal had dreamed with his dad that someday he too would be a prince, the son of the king.

But those dreams were dashed in a day. He could never fulfill the destiny his father had barely inspired him to dream.

It was a strange, scary name for a crippled kid, destined to live the rest of his life with paralyzed feet.

Choosing to Change

Merib-Baal was a name looking to pick a fight.

It's no wonder his first foster mom, his nurse, took him into hiding. At least she did that right.

But even stranger and scarier, the only other man of his family who was not killed was his Uncle Esh-Baal. His uncle refused to fight in the war against the Philistines. Esh-Baal means son of Baal.

That's plain evidence this was a divided family with mixed up priorities.

Two members of the same family: one named Anti Baal; the other, son of Baal.

It sounds like Granddad Saul was trying to cover all the bases with all the gods.

Merib-Baal and Esh-Baal were the only two survivors of the royal family. The Philistine Baal worshipers had defeated Merib-Baal's father, Prince Jonathan, and the children of Is Real.

In the eyes of a five-year-old cripple, there was no way to live up to his name.

Perhaps that's why, while in hiding, he chose to change his name to Mephibosheth.

Enemies Everywhere

Crossing the Jordan River felt safe.

It put some healthy distance between the fugitives and the Philistines. They would not chase very far into a desert of "no green grass."

Merib-Baal grew for the next twenty years, hiding as quietly as possible, eking out a living. He grew up to be anything but a warrior—certainly not a champion. He grew up to be ... handicapped. A victim!

At least the poor foster family took care of him enough, and he found some short-lived happiness as an adult. A young lady agreed to give him her hand in marriage. She even bore him a son.

But don't think for a second that he was living happily ever after. Merib-Baal felt life was unbearable. He and his family could never go back to greener pastures. He had more enemies than just the Philistines.

David was king now in Judah. He was the enemy of Merib-Baal's grandfather, King Saul. When new kings came into power, it was common practice to exterminate every royal family member they could find.

Merib-Baal grew up believing his own people, the people of Is Real, were seeking to destroy him, too.
That meant he could only grow up in relative obscurity and extreme poverty. He would spend his whole life hiding in shame of Baal and in fear of David.

With Prince Jonathan gone, the heir apparent to Grandpa Saul's throne would have been his Uncle Esh-Baal.

Imagine that: the children of the living God, governed by a son of Baal as king.

Bedtime Believer

Can you understand the tears?

Can you understand how a grown man would still cry alone in his room twenty years after being orphaned?

He hoped no one would see him. Oh, his tears weren't so much for himself. After all, a paralyzed man can't expect much in life. And he had reasons to be thankful. His wife fed him every day, and his young son was growing up healthy and with two good feet. Most crippled men didn't even have a wife, much less a son.

But he cried nonetheless. He could never be a complete man to his wife. He could never be a strong champion to his son. He could never provide well for his family, at least not the way he wanted.

What could he give them? He had nothing.

What could he teach his son of life, of God, of Baal? He didn't know himself what he believed.

The evidence was contrary to his father's teaching. What good was his life? What good would it do to believe in God and against Baal?

He fondly remembered Prince Jonathan. He loved his father, even if Jonathan was misguided. Jonathan at least lived with great confidence. He had great joy and happiness, high energy for living, and deep love for people. His father could inspire with bedtime stories of victories that God provided. But now, as much as he loved his dad, lame Merib-Baal believed those teachings to be false.

Those teachings might have been right for his dad, but they weren't right for him.

Poor Little Boy

Merib-Baal could not believe.

Nothing awaited his family but poverty and famine.

When he looked at his wife and son, his heart ached. His wife chose to marry Merib-Baal. He felt sorry for her, but, amazingly enough, that was had been her own decision.

It was different for his son, Micah. He did not choose to be born so poor. His son had no choice in the matter.

His son would never have a future as long as Merib-Baal was his dad.

That's why he gave his son a much more humble name than his own. He gave his son a name that would never cause him trouble.

He named him Micah, which meant "poor little boy."

Dead Dog

The knock that came on the drafty old door confirmed his greatest fear.

It was the day he hoped would never come.

King David had finally found out where he lived. Someone had ratted him out.

Merib-Baal was ordered to be escorted under guard to the palace in Jerusalem.

Merib-Baal had heard recent news that his uncle Esh-Baal had been killed in war against King David.
In finding Merib-Baal, David had tracked down the last of King Saul's royal family. Merib-Baal was the last one. He would die, never living up to his name, having lived a pitiful life.

He was such a loser!

He imagined he would be hung like a criminal, exterminated like the rest of his family, the last of his family line. Well, almost. He could only hope that Micah would be spared. He could only pray they would never discover his only son.

The Song of an Orphan

When Merib-Baal arrived at the palace, he bowed low to honor the king. David could tell he was extremely fearful.

The next words were a shocking surprise. David said, "Don't be afraid. I will show you kindness for the sake of your father, Jonathan. I will restore to you all the land that belonged to your grandfather Saul. You will always eat at my table. You will always eat at the king's royal palace."[24]

Merib-Baal could hardly believe his ears.

Still bowing low, he dared not even lift his head when he said, "What is your servant, that you should even notice a dead dog like me?"

That's as low an opinion as one can have of himself, asking not, "Who is your servant? but "What?"

Then he called himself a dead dog!

Crippled Champion

It was a magnanimous public display of royal pageantry.

King David answered the question publicly by appointing thirty-six servants to work on farm land he gave to Merib-Baal. The servants were to care for his wife and his son Micah, as well. The blessings were abundant.

The crippled Merib-Baal was now like an adopted son to David. He ate every day at the king's table because David loved Prince Jonathan, and King Saul's son loved David.

The Bible says their love for each other surpassed that of love between a man and a woman. The spiritual dimension of God's love between these two was more powerful than sexual love.

Merib-Baal's wife was provided with more than she had ever dreamed, and Micah, the poor little boy, now had his father's servants at his call. A snap of the fingers, a clap of the hands, and he could ask for anything!

Now, he was proud to be the son of Merib-Baal!

The promised victory had been given!

They could now all proudly stand tall and wear the same last name, Against Baal. No longer would a physically crippled father wear a name that hid his royalty. No longer would a spiritually crippled man be ashamed.

But wasn't he the same man?

No, he was changed!

A total transformation took place down deep in his soul, where he hurt the most. His attitude and perspective changed completely to the positive. Merib-Baal lived the rest of his life against Baal, with the same sure confidence of his father. He saw clearly that the worship of Baal, the worship of any idol, was useless.

He received the real victory that was given him, but he knew he had done nothing to earn it. None of these blessings were a result of his efforts.

He was still a cripple, but he was living like a champion!

Father's Friend

Merib-Baal was a new man, a complete man.

For the first time since he was five years old, his life made sense. Now he had the confidence to teach his own son.

The son of Baal was no more. King David defeated the Philistines and the people of Baal. Prince Jonathan's death was avenged.

Merib-Baal now lived in the house of the king who conquered the people of Baal. The name Merib-Baal was a perfect fit in the palace. He belonged there as much as anyone did, as much as any son or child of the king!

What a change his life took when he moved into the house of the king—from poverty to abundance, from an outcast to a child of the king!

He pondered over his father's great love for King David. Could it be that Merib-Baal was named, not after his father, but after his father's best friend, after the king who conquered the people of Baal?

And now he was treated as his adopted son!

Song of Songs

Merib-Baal's servants were unhappy.

After many years of service, they wanted their own land and their own lives. King David was inclined to give it to them, to split the land between the servants and Merib-Baal.

But Merib-Baal gave this answer and advice to David: "Give all the land to my servants!" he said.

"They can have it all, good king! I don't really want the land. All I really want is you. I want the lord of the land. Just let me live in your good grace for the rest of my days! If I have the king and his favor, I have everything I need."

The words inspired the king and touched his heart like no words ever had.

He went to his song book and wrote a new song. He had written hundreds of songs, but this song was special. It was a song of songs.

It would become the greatest, most popular song the king had ever penned.

The song told the king's own story but also the story of Mephibosheth. It also tells your story and mine.

It was "The Song of an Orphan":

The Lord is my shepherd. He's all that I want.

He makes me lie down in green pastures. He leads me beside quiet waters. He restores my soul. He leads me in paths of righteousness for his name's sake.

Though I walk through the darkest valley, even the valley of the shadow of death, I will fear no evil, for You are with me. Your rod and staff comfort me.

You prepare a table before me in the presence of those who were once my enemies. You anoint my head with oil, my cup overflows.

Surely goodness and love will follow me all the days of my life, and I will dwell in the house of the Lord forever.[25]

He Sent His Son

The story of Merib-Baal is a transformational story.

It tells how every one of us is a champion of God's grace. Each of us is born into the royal family of God. God's great plan is for each of us to live as the King's kids. His plan is for each of us to prosper and to eat at His table.[26]

But early in life, we suffer the consequences of sin and a fallen world. Every one of us is influenced by outside factors, powerful negatives beyond our control. It's not really all our fault. We don't know why we were born into a far from perfect family in a far from perfect land. As a result, we are crippled, lame, and handicapped.

We blame God. We blame others. We may even believe for a time that false gods are greater in power than the true and living God.

For a time, we don't know what to believe.

Then we hear false teaching that God is looking for us because he's out to get us. He wants to string us up and hang us.

We go into hiding. We don't want any relationship with God. Our lives lack abundance and blessing. Fear takes away our joy and confidence. Our souls suffer deep poverty.

But our situation is never hopeless.

God made a promise to Prince Jesus that, if He would go after you and me, find us in our hiding place, find us in our despair, then we could come to live with Him.

The good news of the gospel of Jesus Christ is this: God sent His Son to find us!

God's Grace

We think we are hidden.

We hope He can't find us. But we can't escape His relentless pursuit and love.

He finds us. And through Jesus, we are brought into a right relationship with the King, our Heavenly Father. We accept the royal invitation to live in the palace. It's another chance to live again as a child of the King.

Even with our handicap of sin, the favor of God is always there. No matter how bad it seems, accepting the promise of God changes everything. We receive every blessing of salvation, every blessing of this life and the life to come. We become champions of victorious living.

Our Heavenly Father adopts us into His family, but not because of anything we've done. We only believed and accepted the invitation.

In fact, it might be better if we were crippled so we would never think we did anything to earn our free gift of salvation. It's not because of our great works, so we can never brag or boast.

It is by grace we become champions.

Orphans, One and All

When we stand before our God in the judgment, we are all orphans.

We can't hold our earthly parent's hand. We stand alone, as orphans, before our perfect Heavenly Father, just hoping to be adopted.

He's not an earthly father who fails. He's a kind and loving father who wants to sit with us at the table. We accept His daily invitation to His table. We regularly eat with the King.

Let the whole land of Is Real taste and see that the Lord is good!

And all who sing His song from the heart will live with Him forever.

It's your song. It's my song.

It's the Song of an Orphan.

CHAPTER 5

The Little Girl Who Ended a War

It was the last time the sweet little girl would ever see her parents.

Her final terrifying image of her father was of his face just before they beheaded him.

Watching her mom taken away to be abused, she screamed, but her screams did nothing to stop them.

Torn away from her mother's death grip, she would never touch those tender arms again.

It was too much for an eleven-year-old.

Haunted History

The merciless robbers yanked the little girl up on the back of a horse and rode off.

She didn't know where they were taking her, but it was a long trip to a distant land.

As they approached a gate to the city of Damascus, she saw a mound of skulls, piled high beside the road. The vultures were picking and pecking away at some fresh scalps: the hair, the flesh. There were a few bodies with feet or hands cut off, but mostly it was a hill full of dirty, white, boney skulls with empty eye sockets looking all directions for help that never came.

War was a way of life for her people.

History tells us there were thousands of these terrorists in the land of Is Real.

Terrified Terrorist

As merciless as they were, she was still alive.

The young girl became a trophy, a slave in the house of the army commander, Naaman, who was second in power only to the King of Aram. Her life would be spared if she served his wife well. The house where she served was decorated with tokens and treasures from her people.

The little girl baked a fresh batch of chocolate chip cookies as army captains entered the house.

They spoke plans for the next raid of her homeland.

Month after month her head was haunted by visions of the pile of skulls and skeletons. She wondered whether the mound would become a mountain. She wondered how her people could be the people of God.

One day something changed. Naaman, the terrorist, came home … terrified.

During his raids, in which he dealt with death and decay, blood, rot and the filth of war, Naaman contracted a disease on his skin: leprosy.

Highly contagious and deadly, leprosy was worse than any disease in America today. It made those it attacked look horrible; it caused them to lose their fingers and toes—and even their noses!

There was no high-powered prescription medication to delay symptoms and slow its advance. There was no way to keep the disease secret and go on with life for twenty more years.

Even the doctors did not want to examine a leper.

"Stay away!" they shouted.

"We can see from a distance what you have. There's nothing we can do!"

"It's incurable!"

Love for a Leper

For all practical purposes, Naaman was finished.

In a few days he'd give up his post as commander and be an outcast.

His wife could never safely embrace him again. He wondered whether she would even engage in conversation at night.

Now he knew how the little girl felt, the one who would never again be held or hugged.

He was untouchable.

The ruthless soldier cried like a baby at home, when no one watched. No one except a little slave girl.

It would be natural for her to have vengeful thoughts. It served him right, this godless army commander. Her God would see justice done. He would pay for his deeds in a slow, agonizing death, unless he preferred to fall on his sword.

But the little girl wondered what would happen to her.

Would she be required to take care of him in his illness? Would she, too, contract leprosy as she washed his clothes and changed his bedding? Or would he leave while she was transferred to the house of another soldier? Would she be abused? Would she end up on Skull Mountain?

Her parents had not left her defenseless.

They gave her the greatest protection any parents can give their children when they leave home: they left her in the hands of God.

They taught her that, no matter what bad things happened, no matter the circumstances or the war, her God was a God of love. He could be trusted in the worst situations. He was a God of power and healing.

The bandits took her away from her parents and her home, but they never took God and His love out of her heart.

From Horror to Hope

Naaman cupped his drooping head in his hands as he sobbed.

Suddenly, he felt a gentle hand on his shoulder.

He looked up through his tears.

The little girl told Naaman, "You should make a trip to see the preacher in the land of Is Real. He will cure you of your leprosy."[27]

She had a rare case of child-like faith, the kind of faith Jesus said is easier to find in children.

Naaman did the same thing you and I would do in his shoes. He would do whatever it takes!

He went to the king for permission to travel to the land of Is Real, not to capture slaves this time, not to bring back bounty, but to be saved.

The king sent Naaman, his army general, with a half-ton of gold and silver. He sent a royal letter respectfully requesting some supernatural cure.

Flabbergasted

The alarm sounded from one town to the next.

Naaman traveled through the land of Is Real, escorted by his army of soldiers. The bandits were on the march again, unchallenged, unopposed.

The people of Is Real were surprised, though, when no attack came. Naaman's was a peaceful advance, which was strange behavior according to homeland security. Word got out that Naaman's army was heading for Elisha's house because the commander had leprosy.

Hundreds of horses and chariots already surrounded Elisha's house when the commander pulled up to the front door.

Naaman intended to introduce himself as commander of the great army of Aram. They would recognize his name instantly. They would know his power and the wars he had won. He planned to seal the deal by offering great wealth in exchange for healing power.

But before Naaman could dismount his horse and knock on the door to make his offer, a messenger came out and gave instructions, "Go wash yourself seven times in the Jordan, and you will be healed."[28]

The door closed.

No introduction. No chit chat. No hospitality. No buttering up. No flattery. No royal treatment. No preacher.

No "get to know God" sermon.

Naaman was flabbergasted.

Trusting a Child

"What do you make of that?" Naaman thought.

"Is this some kind of joke to embarrass and humiliate me in front of my whole army? A little girl sends me on a wild goose chase to a far-away preacher, and when I get here, he's too busy to come to the front door.

"I bring millions in gold and silver, and the preacher shows no interest! Who am I dealing with here?

"If I'm going to die, can't I at least have a little dignity and respect from those I've conquered? Doesn't anything I've done matter? Do these people know who I am?

"For the first time in my life, I need help, and some nobody comes out to give me a message that makes no earthly sense!

"'Go jump in the river!' they say. 'Wash seven times! You'll be healed!'

"Yeah right, and if I do that on this, my final expedition, it's how my army remembers me forever.

"Must I also face losing my legacy? It's all I have left! It looks like I came all this way for nothing.

"How foolish of me to trust a little slave girl!"

Command for a Commander

Naaman thought it was nonsense.

He became enraged. He thought the preacher would surely come out and call on the name of the Lord, his God, wave his hand over the spot, and cure him of his leprosy. "Instead," Naaman thought, "all he does is tell me to go jump in the river. We have rivers at home!"

The commander wasn't comfortable taking commands. Not a command like this.

For a moment, Naaman thought how easy it would be to fight one more battle in the ongoing war. He could go out with a bang! Naaman could swing his sword in anger and go down in history as a fighting hero.

But his soldiers came to him and said, "Think again. If the preacher had told you to do some great work, you would do it. If you were told to slay a dragon, you would go. If you were asked to build a temple to his God, you were prepared to pay for it.

"But he asked you to do no work, pay no price. Just dip in the cool water and be washed. We came all this way. Here we are and there's the water.

"Don't worry what people think. Don't be humiliated. Be humble. Give up your pride. Do what he said."

For the first time ever, Naaman disarmed in enemy territory.

Then he went down the river bank and dipped himself in the Jordan seven times, as the preacher told him.

His skin was restored and became as clean as that of—an eleven-year-old child.

Peace without Pay

Naaman looked at his skin.

Standing there in his skivvies, dripping wet, he cried out in elation.

His army watched as he jumped up and down on the edge of the river bank, splashing his happiness and relief into the air.

Compelled by the joy of his salvation, he went back, still dripping wet, to Elisha's house, demanding to meet the unseen messenger he never even met. As Naaman sat in his underwear on his horse, Elisha came out to meet him.

Naaman shouted, "Now I know there is no God in all the world except in the land of Is Real! Please accept a gift from your servant."

Elisha answered, "I serve the Lord. You can't pay me. I will not accept anything in exchange for your salvation. I didn't give it to you."

Elisha wanted Naaman and all his army who witnessed the power of God that day to know that you can't negotiate your own terms with the Lord.

Blessing and healing come when we trust and obey.

When it comes to mercy, you can't buy it. Money will do you no good.

When it comes to salvation, you can't earn it. Work will do no good. You can only receive it.

History tells us that, at least for a time, there was no more war.

Peace reigned in the land.

Cookies and Kindness

Alone in the kitchen, the little eleven-year-old slave girl sang quietly to herself as she baked chocolate chip cookies for the commander's wife.

She set some back for the commander to eat when he came home. She wondered how things were going for him.

She also wondered when her life would get better. Would she end up on Skull Mountain? Would God come to save her?

She didn't know that He had already come to her rescue. The world around her was already changed. Her future was completely transformed.

By showing mercy to an army general, she hoped to receive mercy from him, and she did.

Countries, commanders, and kings could not change what one little girl did with God on her side.

This time, when the army returned to Damascus, no skulls or scalps were tossed on the mound.

A forgotten little girl, long presumed dead, ended years of war between nations by sharing her God.

Nothing is impossible with God!

Jesus said that, to experience heaven, we must become like this little girl, ruled by a positive faith.

Bitterness makes war with God and with the world, but this little girl, through an act of kindness, made peace with her enemies.

Peace for the world!

Cross of Calvary

It's the same road.

Today, on the road from Damascus to Jerusalem, by the side of the road approaching the city gate is a hideous-looking hill in the shape of a skull.

Eight-hundred fifty years after Naaman, Jesus carried a cross outside that city gate, the Damascus gate. On that road and on that very hill He would be crucified.

There would be no mercy for Him at the place of the skull, Golgotha, where skeletons marked the ground.

In Hebrew, Golgotha was a ghoulish term, conjuring up images of goblins and ghosts. If there were a Hebrew Halloween, parents would never let their children go there.

However, over time, the love of our Savior, Jesus Christ, overpowered that cross and that hill, those symbols of death and punishment.

People all over the world now wear a cross to represent unconditional love.

Today the cross is a thing of beauty, and the term Golgotha in Hebrew has been traded for a beautiful Latin word, Calvary.

Slaying Self

Here's the hardest part.

It's right up there with slaying a dragon. It's the hardest thing ever to put away all excuses, to give up pride and become humble before God—humble enough to simply believe and obey before it's too late.

Don't put it off.

God used Naaman for years to punish the land of Is Real because they were more godless and wicked than Aram.

Jesus made religious people angry when He said, "There were many lepers in Is Real, but none were healed; only Naaman the leper."[29]

Why?

Naaman became receptive. His heart was open.

Even in their desperate condition, the lepers in Is Real would not believe they could be healed.

So they stayed lost.

What about us? Are we receptive? Are we able to turn what is so difficult into something easy?

Are we able to receive a simple message from God through children?

Chapter 6

Running Away Naked

A twelve-year-old boy was out on the streets in the middle of the night.

He was a gangster "wannabe".

His parents didn't know where he was. If they had known, they would not have approved. If they had known the authorities would be called in, they would have supervised him more closely.

Had they known their son would be in trouble with the law, maybe they could have steered him in a different direction before it was too late.

Sneaking Out Sagging

He was hanging around a rough crowd, the wrong friends.

Two gangs were meeting in the dark. There were weapons involved—clubs and blades. Both sides were ready to slash, cut, and shoot.

Some kids can't even go to a PG-13 movie without their parents, much less be involved in real violence and bloodshed. It was no place for a kid, out way past his bedtime. He should have been in bed asleep.

If kids are going to live long, they need to establish a healthy way of living while they are young. They need safe routines and boundaries and close parental supervision if they are going to stay out of trouble.

Although his parents knew all that, they still could not stop all the bad stuff that went down that night.

They had sent him to bed. He put on the long nightshirt that he slept in and kissed his mother and father goodnight.

Then, without even putting on any underclothes, he grabbed a couple of his mother's chocolate chip cookies, climbed out the window, and took off.

His nightshirt came down to his knees, so when he caught up with the gang, he fit right in with their droopy, sagging clothes.

But his were draftier than theirs.

Followers and Leaders

The boy followed the gang to the city park, where they were supposed to meet the other gang.

Why was he even there? He was much younger than the rest of them. He had no business there at the park. Was it because he just didn't want to obey his parents all the time?

What is it that makes a young kid a "wannabe"?

He knew that, if his mother knew where he was, she'd have a fit, and his dad would never trust him out on his own again.

But the kid also knew this was big stuff. What was happening was big news that would be in the front page headlines of the newspaper. He couldn't tell his parents.

The leader had called his gang together. They weren't backing down to anyone, especially not the other gang.

The boy wasn't invited, but neither was he going to miss out.

All Hyped Up

On the way to the park, he followed quietly behind everyone else.

He didn't want the older gang members to send him home. They were used to wannabes hanging around, but he was careful, taking no chances.

He observed and listened as the nervous leader talked of sure victory. The best the boy could figure out, they were all upset about one of their gang member's defecting to the other side. It wasn't cool.

Following along in the shadows, the boy watched the gang spread out in the park. They had been there before. They made themselves comfortable as if it were their regular hangout.[30]

He waited, but nothing much seemed to be happening. He was surprised and even a little disappointed that some of the gang members fell asleep after a while.

Maybe he was wrong. Nothing was really going to happen. Maybe the story was all hyped up. You know how it goes sometimes.

But he wasn't about to take a nap out under the stars. Not this early. He had never sneaked out this way before.

He was so shot full of adrenaline that his little heart pumped way too strong to sleep.

Face Off

The gang leader came twice to wake up the members.

He fussed with them for sleeping. The boy was proud that he had stayed awake and outdone some of the older ones. He saw the leader look over at him and smile as if he approved.

For a moment, he felt big.

Maybe the leader thought he had what it took to be a gang member, but it was dark and he wasn't really sure why the leader was smiling at him.

The boy didn't know what was going on, and it was shaping up to be a boring night. Soon after the leader smiled at him, even he became sleepy.

Just as his eyes were about to close, he heard a noise in the distance. Looking up, he saw some lights flickering. What appeared to be a mob procession of torches and lanterns came over the hill into the park. The cadence of marching soldiers sent another shot of adrenaline into his veins.

The leader ordered, "Everybody up! Here comes the defector!"

The boy stepped back a little as the gang members rose to their feet and lined up. It was apparent there was going to be a fight, but they were greatly outnumbered and out-armored. The boy wondered how they would respond since they had vowed they wouldn't back down to anyone.

The night lit up with torches; the boy could see the huge mob clearly now.

The two gangs faced each other.

A familiar voice spoke to the leader.

"Hey, old friend! Good to see you!"

They embraced each other and kissed. There was something weird about it. The defector acted as though he hadn't seen the gang leader in a long time.

The mob with all their weapons, were no longer sure they were facing off for a fight.

First to Fall

The boy had seen his gang holding only two swords.

The leader had said that was enough.[31]

Both swords were hidden from view in the gang members' baggy clothes. Any fighting with the well-armed mob they faced wouldn't be a fair fight.

And his gang wasn't a dangerous-looking bunch of thugs. They looked more like a small group of men out in their night clothes.

The leader stepped forward and spoke to the guards in an unthreatening way. "Who you looking for?" he asked in a friendly, helpful tone.

"Your leader!" they answered.

He raised a gentle hand to the shoulder of the guard and with a big smile said, "I'm your hullaballoo!"

The soldiers in front acted surprised and stepped backward as they fumbled for their swords. They stumbled over the soldiers behind them. Some got all tangled up and even fell to the ground.[32]

The boy thought it was funny, but he didn't dare laugh out loud.

He was amazed that his gang's leader was so cool.

The other guys were falling fast, like dominoes.

An Ear to Hear

No damage was done, and the guards got back up on their feet. Then, slowly, the guards began to circle the gang.

Again the boy's leader asked, "Who did you say you're searching for?"

"We're looking for Jesus!"

He answered like he wasn't worried. "I'm right here!"

Suddenly one of the gang members, Simon, drew a sword he was hiding inside his robe. He took aim. He reared back to decapitate one of the only unarmed members of the mob. He took the first swing. He struck the first blow. He tried to take off the man's head.

The man, only a servant, ducked just in time, but his right ear dropped to the ground out in the middle of everyone. A split-second later, the servant fell. Blood trickled between the man's fingers as he moaned with pain.

Before anything else could happen, before anyone could retaliate, Jesus turned to Simon and grabbed him. It's a good thing he acted so fast, as it's hard to see how Simon could have survived what he had coming from the rival gang.

It looked as though Jesus' quick thinking saved all of his gang members from being killed right there in a fight. A brief moment allowed everyone to see what the leader would do.

After all, the guards weren't attacked. They figured the only one hurt was one of the guys from the land of Is Real. The servant was one of the defector's people. The guards were in no hurry to risk their lives over what was primarily a family feud, a domestic quarrel.

They were willing to wait a second. There was no apparent need for a fight since the leader was now holding back the gang. He was acting to make more bloodshed unnecessary.

He was acting to save the gang.

Jesus ordered Peter to put his sword away.

Miraculous Moment

Reaching down to the ground, Jesus picked up the ear.

Blood was peppered with dirt. He stared for a moment at the organ in his hand. No one moved.

The ear had a hole in the middle, as if someone had driven a huge nail through it. He could see the flesh of his hand through the bloody hole.

And now, if you can believe what the twelve-year-old boy saw next, you can believe anything.

He saw Jesus turn to the spattered, squealing servant, holding his head. He saw Jesus actually put the ear back on the servant's head. It reattached immediately.

He saw it!

Healed, the servant rose from the pool of blood.

It was clear to all that, even though he was supposed to be in the group against Jesus, he was thankful.

Seeing and Believing

The boy remembered that it was stories like this one that started the gang in the first place.

That's why he slipped out of the house that night.

He was hanging around in the shadows and following this leader he had heard so much about.

People had said, "We guarantee that if you just hang around Jesus long enough, you'll be amazed!"

That's why the boy was a "wannabe."

No sir, there was nothing boring about all this. This time, the twelve-year-old boy had seen it for himself.

He had done the right thing, sneaking out of the house.

He had no regrets.

Fast Forward

Then reality snapped back into the guards.

They were on a mission. They had orders. They would lose their heads if they did not return with Jesus in custody.

"We're taking you in!" one guard said.

"Why?" the leader objected. "Am I some dangerous criminal?"

They grabbed Jesus, and as soon as they did, Simon took off running. Then the whole gang, every one of them, took off in all directions, running into the darkness.

The guards chased them. It was crazy for a moment, but they didn't catch anyone except the leader.

He never ran.

It all happened so fast. Then the boy realized that, to see the medical miracle, he had moved in a little too close, and now he was the only one left standing where the gang had been.

A couple of guards grabbed him, one on each side. They had him now, a firm grip on each shoulder of his night shirt. They ripped his shirt and roughed him up a little as they lined him up to follow behind Jesus.

He would be escorted right along behind Jesus to face the authorities.

He was in more trouble than he'd ever been in his life. It was a desperate situation and he needed to get away.

He thought of his parents and how he should have never crept out that window.

Then Jesus turned to look back over His shoulder at the boy. He smiled that same approving grin the boy thought he had seen earlier.

Jesus nodded and winked at the boy, as if to say, "Everything is going to be okay! Do what you must!"

Then the guard poked at Jesus and barked, "You there! Turn around, face forward. March!"

It was almost as if Jesus turned back toward the boy on purpose because, when the guard reached toward Jesus, his grip on the boy loosened just a little.

It was just enough for the boy to duck through his baggy nightshirt and slip away. The guards held firmly to his shirt, but the boy was gone. He took off and, boy, could he run!

It didn't matter that he was naked now.

He was getting away.

Worldwide Wannabes

Once in the darkness, he ran faster than he had ever run in his life.

Clothed now, only in the darkness of night he made his way through the shadows of the park. He found the darkest parts of the street corners and alleys, moving from bush to tree.

Running Away Naked

Out of breath, he panted heavily, but he couldn't stop running away—or we should say, running home.

It was a strange predicament, he thought, to be running home ... to his parents ... as fast as he could ... naked.

Finally, he saw his house up ahead. He wondered whether his parents would know he had been out all night. He had never sneaked out before, and he vowed he would never do it again. He'd learned his lesson.

His mother was right.

He crawled back in the window in such a hurry he scraped his knees, arms, and legs.

He sat on the edge of his bed and checked over his cuts and bruises. He pulled on a new nightshirt and slipped under the covers. They felt so warm.

It all happened so fast that he couldn't believe it when he saw that the sun was beginning to come up.
He was exhausted.

Just as he was getting to sleep, his mother came in to wake him. She said sternly, "I know what you were up to last night." She began picking up his clothes and straightening his room.

"You do?" he asked.

Without even looking at him, she said, "Yes, I do, and I'm not very happy with you."

"I'm sorry!" he said, bursting into tears.

He grabbed his mother and buried his face in her apron. He held on to her tightly. He had never held her so strongly or sobbed so loudly.

She held him as he cried. His dad came in to see what all the commotion was about. "What's going on in here?" he asked his wife, hardly noticing his son.

The mother said, "Oh, it's nothing, Honey. I just caught John Mark with his hands in the cookie jar. He was into the cookies again last night."

His dad said, "Is that all? It seems like there must be more to it than that, the way he's carrying on. Are you sure that's all, John Mark?"

The boy said, "Yes, there's more to it. I can't talk about it right now. If it's okay with you, I'll write it all down for you."

And now you know the story of John Mark, the naked runaway[33] who wrote the Gospel of Mark, the Good News of Jesus Christ that to this very day makes people all over the world into "wannabes."

Chapter 7

A Way-Out Teenager

A teenager held her father in one arm, her mother in the other.

The mother held the teen's newborn baby brother.

Their weeping was restrained and muffled so as not to disturb the sleeping child.

They were out of time. The authorities were coming to take the infant.

"What will you do, Father?" the girl asked.

Calmly, sadly, he said, "I'll fight them."

"But Father, if you fight them, they will kill you."

"Yes," he said, "I see no other way."

Unplanned Pregnancy

"But Father, after they kill you, they will kill my baby brother. Why should we lose both of you?"

She turned to her mother. "Mother, isn't there something we can do?"

The anguished mother said, "When they come, if I hold on to the baby, they will only tear him apart. Then my own hands will be the cause of his death. I could not bear it. I will give the baby to them and look the other way. If the child is to be destroyed, I will not look. Otherwise, I will never be able to see anything else for the rest of my life."

They huddled together, tears streaming from one face to another. It was the beginning of a long, sleepless night.

The baby had been born at the worst possible time.
She hadn't planned her pregnancy.

But there is really no such thing as an unplanned pregnancy.

It was God's plan.

Let Go and Let God

Pharoah had given his edict, a law for which he would be forever remembered. Every baby boy born of a slave family was to be taken and killed.[34]

For months now, the teenage girl had thought about this situation. She wondered whether there was another plan.

She prayed. She schemed. And she thought she saw a way out.

"Mother," she said, "when I go to the Great River to serve Pharoah's daughter, I've heard her say how much she loves babies. She dreams that she will one day be the mother of many children.

"As she bathes in the river, she sings children's songs. She says she's never seen a baby she didn't love. She says she can't wait to have her own. She even wants to adopt.

"Mother, what if she found my brother in the Great River? What if we put him in a basket in the river reeds, where the current could not take him, right next to where Bithiah bathes? She would be sure to find him when he cries. What if she looked into his baby eyes and fell in love? What if she decided to adopt him and let him live?"

The mother bit back in tears. "What if! What if! What if!" she cried. "Miriam, what if the current does take him down the river? What if he drowns in the Nile? What if the crocodiles eat him before he even sinks to the bottom?"

"But, Mother, I can see it happening! I know the river! I know Bithiah!

"We have no choice. We have to hope. We can't just wait for the soldiers to come with their swords and spears. If we wait, it will be too late! Mother, you yourself said you must not hold on to the baby. If you hold on, you will kill him yourself. We must let go. We must give this plan a chance. I have prayed with all my heart, and I believe God has given me this vision."

Love's Logic

That night, the mother took tar and pitch from the slave pits. She smeared it around and inside a small basket and then spread soft cloth over it.

As the sun came up, with the soldiers on their way, the exhausted parents prayed and kissed their baby good-bye.

Miriam went with her mother to take her baby brother down to the Great River, where she regularly attended Bithiah during her morning bath.

Miriam placed the basket securely in the reeds, making sure it was not going to get loose and drift out into the moving water. The mother walked home with the greatest fear and greatest hope.

Miriam waited for Bithiah and prayed. She believed love would find a way to resolve the situation. In her short few years on earth, she knew love to be the greatest force on earth—stronger than fear, more powerful than hate. She knew love connects across international boundaries, that love overcomes racial, ethnic, and class bias.

Love was the only power that could withstand the King's great edict.

The Adoption Option

"Oh, look, Bithiah!" Miriam said innocently. "There's a sound coming from the river reeds, and there's something caught over there."

"Yes, Miriam!" Bithiah exclaimed. "It looks like a basket, and it sounds like a baby. Go get it and bring it here. Let's see what it is!"

When Miriam brought the basket and lifted the cover, Pharoah's daughter instantly loved the baby. Just as Miriam had predicted, Bithiah was not about to let this opportunity pass.

She said, "From this day forward, this lost, abandoned baby belongs to me. The king will let me keep him!" Only Bithiah had the power and provisions to save this helpless little life.

At the same time, Pharoah's daughter, for all her wealth and power, knew something else.

She knew she wasn't ready to become a mother. She wasn't prepared to lose her freedom—not yet anyway, not like a real mother. She wasn't ready to take on the tasks that true motherhood requires.

She had to be honest with herself.

Bithiah knew she had no business taking care of a baby by herself, so when Miriam offered to find a mature Hebrew mother to suckle the baby,35 Pharoah's daughter suspected what had happened.

She knew what Miriam was doing, but she was in love with the baby, and she chose to save his life.

They all chose the path of adoption.

Mother to Mother

Miriam skipped home that morning, singing.

She found her mother and father wrapped in each other's arms, waiting for news of their son's fate, their tears still flowing. Their greatest fears were mingled with faith.

Then their sobbing turned into screams of laughter and tears of joy. They huddled and jumped and spun each other around the room in a dance.

What relief! What unspeakable joy!

Miriam urged her mother to come to the palace to provide nourishment for her son—the son who had once been as good as dead.

A resurrection took place in her heart.

She would nurse him for three more years.

All she had to do to save her son's life was go along with Bithiah's plan for adoption.

To bless her son, she had to believe. She had to believe in something greater than herself. She had to believe that adoption was very much God's own good plan.

We can only wonder what those three years were like for the birth mother. Every day she nursed her own child, named by another woman. Strange and foreign as the other woman was, she, too, loved the boy. And she had the power to save him.

The mother knew she would have to give him up again. As he went daily back and forth between two mothers, she gave him up again and again and again. For the sake of her child's life, she had to push down the resentment, to put away all jealousy!

Was it difficult? Perhaps. Perhaps not.

When faced with the sobering choices of reality, mature love finds it easy to do the right thing.

Plan for a Prince

The birth mother remembered her words.

If she held on to her son too tightly, her own hands would destroy him. With her, he had no future. With her, he would grow up a slave, impoverished, saddled with a life of hard labor.

Or he wouldn't grow up at all.

If she found the courage and peace to let him go, he had a chance in life; a great chance.

A kid just needs a chance to be a champion.

What good would a mother's selfish love do in this situation? Another mother might reason that her son would be better off dead, thinking, "If I can't have him, no one else can either."

But love does not think of its own feelings. Even in great pain and overwhelming fear, Miriam's mother put aside her feelings for herself and did what was best for her child.

By letting go, she ensured that Moses would grow up with a lifetime of protection and benefits. He would have a life his birth parents could never provide.

By setting her son free, Moses' mother was setting herself free in an unselfish way. She would receive God's blessing for doing the right thing for her son.

Adoption is God's "way out" to freedom and blessing. The blessing birth mothers find when they let go in the adoptive process is the blessing of freedom: freedom from becoming a slave for life, and freedom from a lifetime of frustration, freedom from failing to give a child the best life possible.

An unplanned pregnancy fits right into someone else's prayers and plans. Every time one dream ends, God provides a way to dream again.

In the life of every Christian, adoption has always been part of God's plan.[36]

Adoption turns an unplanned pregnancy into a prince.

Tempted, Not Trapped

The name Moses means "drawn out."

The name signifies his salvation when he was drawn out of the water. God's promise is to always provide a way out of any bad situation. We will never have to endure more than we can.[37]

For every person surrounded by evil circumstances, there is an answer. There is always another way out of any nightmare situation. Any mixed-up combination of unexpected events beyond our control has a back door.

We must look for the exit sign.

God provides the door, and He opens it, too. When confronted with evil, we run to and through the exit. Finding the way out is our victory. We triumph over the enemy.[38]

Everyone is tempted. No one is trapped.

Parent or Pharoah

Growing up, the best lesson Moses ever learned was the one his mother and sister lived and preached: Let the child go. Set him free, or you will destroy him.

Healthy love sets the other person free.

Moses preached it to. He preached the same sermon to Pharoah about the children of Is Real.

"Let my people go! Slavery destroys any people! One person can never completely own another without destroying him or her."

As it goes for Pharoahs, it goes for parents, too.

When parents own their children, they cannot do them right.

Every life is created free to belong to God.

Far Out, Way Out

Moses is one of the leaders of the Bible.

Adoption turned his life around. So did his sister.

Perhaps because she is female, we overlook another great hero. Perhaps because she is a child, we miss a great champion.

Perhaps because a child's faith sometimes looks easy, we take her for granted.

Miriam's early heroic faith as a teenager is overshadowed by the legend her brother became eighty years later. But long before Moses saved the people of Is Real, a teenage girl saved him.

Miriam acted in faith. She had the vision without which her brother and her people would have perished.

When she was only a child, she became a champion in the land of Is Real.

History got it right, however. Thousands of years later, the records still honor Miriam as a leader of Is Real. She is right up there with her brothers Moses and Aaron.[39]

Without Miriam, there would have been no freedom for her people.

When she was only a teenager, she taught her mother and Moses to look for God's far-out way out.

Chapter 8

Goliath Faces the Giant

Two armies faced each other on opposing mountains.
In the valley below, a trickling creek bed drew a line in the sand.

For the two nations and two races of people, co-existence was out of the question.

The inevitable day of slaughter drew near.

Meanwhile, miles away on a peaceful mountainside, a shepherd boy played his harp and echoed praise through the canyon—praise to his Lord for protection and provision.

Tens of thousands of soldiers postured and prepared to destroy each other.

One nation had a clear advantage.

The people of God were outnumbered, out-armed, and outsized.[40]

At the same time, a scrawny teenager, all alone in the hills, fought a lion that had a lamb in its mouth.

He killed that lion, and then he thanked his Lord.

Unless the people of Is Real could accept terms of slavery, their lives would end.

They found themselves in a supersized land, up against giants.[41] One slept in a bed more than thirteen feet long.[42]

Their champion fighter, Goliath, wore 125 pounds of armor and was nine feet tall.[43]

Across the range, a five-foot-nothing kid killed a bear that was attacking his flock.

He gave thanksgiving and glory to God for his victory.

Cheese from a Champion

For forty days, Goliath stood out in front of his army and taunted his enemy.

"You don't all want to die, do you? Let your champion come out and fight me in a winner-take-all match. Whoever is on the losing team can surrender and live."

The men all ran away.

Far away, a concerned old father sat on the front porch. He felt useless for battle, but he prayed, and he wondered what he could do to help his sons. It was only a little thing, the smallest thing, he thought, but it was something. All he had to offer was some fresh little cheeses.

He called for his youngest boy, David, to deliver food to his older brothers at the battle front.

Cheese, bread, and grain.

The father's small act of service set in motion a chain of events that made all the difference in the war.

David took the food and left it at the supply line.

Then he broke the rules.

Running to the battle front to see his brothers, he took provisions only a champion can deliver.

Confidence, courage, and faith!

Belonging in Battle

When David arrived at the battle front, three messengers opposed him.

The first message was sent by his oldest brother.

Eliab was surprised to hear his youngest brother was at the front line, running around the soldiers.

Like a typical kid, David had all kinds of questions. What's going on? Who is this Goliath? We're not scared of him, are we?

What could be more irritating than a little brother asking a hundred questions when the older brother is focused on fear?

Eliab burned with anger and fired back questions of his own. Why have you come here? Who is taking care of your little herd of sheep? You are so conceited and wicked! You just came to watch the battle, didn't you?"[44]

Some men are defeated by a question, destroyed by a doubt.

But doubts don't defeat giants!

Eliab was a common negative messenger of the kind we often face: our own family.

"Why have you come down here?" Eliab asked his brother.

Translation: You don't belong in battle.

Sending Children to War

Family members mean well, but they handicap their children with this kind of message.

Mothers say, "You will always be my little child. Even when you're twenty, thirty, forty years old, you'll still be my baby." Dads say, "Don't go into ministry or mission work. It's a tough way to make a living."

It's a big mistake when we don't encourage one another, especially our own children, to grow up and go into battle to:
- defy peer pressure
- listen to the right music
- live a moral life when others don't
- avoid drugs and keep their language clean
- live with manners, respectful and responsible
- do what is right when no one is watching
- stand up to friends who want to lead us astray.

This is a battle only for giants!

We too seldom have ears to hear Psalms 127:3-5: "Children are a reward from the Lord. Like arrows in the hands of a warrior are sons born in one's youth. Blessed is the man whose quiver is full of them. They will not be put to shame when they contend with their enemies."

Children are made for battle.

Champion or Chump

Children are created to grow up strong.

The family is where they should be sharpened and prepared for battle when they leave home.

Any school administrator or teacher will tell you it's a common parental problem. Parents say, "No My child never does wrong! No one should discipline my child. School is no place for a battle. The home is no place for conflict."

Note to families: Get over yourself before you destroy the ones you love. The school is a good place to teach children spiritual character-building. The home is a safe place to wrestle with values. Our families are where we struggle and, yes, "fight" with our kids over the life choices they make.

Yes, it's tough.

Families take it too easy when they give little children a free pass to misbehave or be rude. It's easy to laugh at little smart-alecks at home and say, "Aren't they cute?"

How will they behave in public then?

Yes, our children should be able to "let their hair down," relax and make mistakes, especially at home. But even at home there should be a line drawn. Easy street doesn't prepare children to be champions. It prepares them to be chumps and losers.

Chores for Champions

How does a parent raise a child to be a giant, a champion?

David's father, Jesse, started out by giving him the family chores.

That is something every parent can do!

Goliath Faces the Giant

David was sent to do a man's work when he was only a teenager. Jesse put him in charge and sent him out to the hills to protect, feed, and save the sheep.

There, David faced a lion and a bear.

Jesse did not send David to face the lion and bear; he sent him to do the chores. Mowing the lawn has its risks. The tractor is dangerous. The milk cow kicks. A power saw requires proper training. There are rattlesnakes out on the farm.

The hills require homework. Jesse prepared his son. By giving him chores, he taught his son that he expected him to become a man. He taught him the dangers and gave him protection. He taught him to have faith, to be brave, and to trust God.

Jesse didn't protect David to the point of handicapping him.

After David passed the test, Jesse sent him to the place of battle.

Now, those are some family chores that will teach anyone to trust God! What parent in his or her right mind would do such a thing? What kind of parent is that?

The kind who raises a king!

Whatever Is Worthy

Eliab asked, "With whom did you leave those few sheep in the desert?"

Translation: Get back to your usual place and pecking order in the family.

Unfortunately, brothers and sisters, parents and families who give this message keep young people from being their best.

Many children, no matter how long they live, never go higher than their parents did. "Well," they say, "that's the way we were raised in our family. Mom was on drugs, so I'll probably take that same path. What was good enough for her is good enough for me. My family was poor so I'll be poor. Dad was alcoholic, so I guess I'll be one too. He went to prison, so that's where I'll end up."

It's hard to go farther than our upbringing, but great parents want their kids to do better. They teach children to think independently, to engage in higher thinking, to be God's giants.

Whatever is excellent or praiseworthy, God's Giant thinks diligently on such things.[45]

Family Fear

David wasn't defeated by the first two questions, so Eliab landed his biggest blow.

"I know you. Your heart is wicked and conceited. You only want to watch the battle."

Translation: "You care only about yourself. You care nothing for your family."

There are various versions of this message: Don't act like you are better than us. Don't judge us. Do you think we are lost?

When a family member questions our motives, it pierces the heart. Many adults and children are defeated at this point. They say, "I know the Bible says one thing, but my parents say another. My brother and sister don't want me to become a Christian. If I take a strong stand, my family will think I'm against them."

False accusations! Faulty assumptions!
All based on fear!

Jesus wants the best for our families. He wants us to show them a better way and a higher love. We never abandon our brothers and sisters. We never reject our children or parents.

By rising above, by rising to the challenges and pursuing our best lives, we help our families fight the battle. We show the way, and everyone wins. We become part of a winning team that includes every member of our families.

Like it or not, every one of us is involved in spiritual battle. Some kids disobey their parents and sneak off to parties. Other kids disobey and sneak off to church.

Many young Christians lead their parents to victory in Christ. Like David, they turn the greatest blessing of life back on their families.

The fear of family battle raises questions and doubts. The fear is as real and strong as facing a mountain—or a mountain lion.

But fear can also be imaginary, and it vanishes into thin air when it is faced with faith, courage, and confidence.

Able, Above All

God's giant then had to get past a second negative messenger, the reigning champion.

King Saul told David, "You can't go out against this Philistine and fight him; you are only a boy, and he has been a fighting man since his youth. You are not able."

Afraid to fight Goliath, Saul decided to send David out to face Goliath anyway, and he showed he was a washed up "has been." Saul's offer of the king's own armor was nothing but camouflage for his cowardice. His help would only weigh David down.

The reigning champion was saying, "You will have to wear all the armor I wore. Use my sword, my helmet. Fight my style. No, you are not really able to do this job. I'm here to help you any way I can, but let's face it: you don't really have what it takes."

God's giant must get past the reigning champion, the previous manager, the former preacher.

Watch out for trainers who have stopped growing. Be careful around those who have given up progressing. Those who don't really believe in you may hold you back with these common words: "This is the way we do it here. I've been here a long time. No one knows this place better than I do. If you expect to be successful, you need to do it my way. To have any chance at all, here is what you do."

Such people may be great and may have tremendous command of authority. Their knowledge may be vast, and they may have accomplished much good. But a negative put-down about our ability to fight the battle is not from God.

God's giant ignores such "stinking thinking" and moves forward anyway!

The giant treats the reigning champion with respect, but he knows "God put me in this position!"

The message a giant believes comes from God.

"We're children of the true King. We're more than able to handle anything we can imagine, ask, or think."[46]

Going with God

Friendly fire can be demoralizing, but God uses it to train and prepare for ultimate victory.

If you've not allowed these first two messengers to defeat you, if you've ignored every negative statement made to hold you back, then you have already defeated a lion and a bear!

You're ready to face the third messenger, Goliath.

Goliath, too, wanted to defeat David with words. He hoped to intimidate the teenager and get him to surrender without a fight. But he was surprised when young David came running out to meet him with no armor and no weapons Goliath could see.

David saw Goliath and sized him up.

He thought, "Goliath is slower than a lion, he's not as strong as a bear, and he's too big to miss! With God on my side, how can I lose?"

Loser's Look

They stood fairly close.

Goliath "looked David over and saw he was only a boy, ruddy and handsome, and he despised him."

Poor guy! He was jealous of David's youth and good looks!

Even a Goliath can have a chink in his armor, a crack in his mental outlook!

Paul told Timothy years later, "Don't let anyone look down on you because you are young."[47]

Do you think someone is unable because of their youth and inexperience? Do you disqualify them because of their age?

Are they unqualified on a technicality? Make sure you don't hold them back. Don't be a giant stumbling block.

Goliath said to David, "Am I a dog that you come at me with sticks?" and the Philistine cursed David by his gods. "Come here," he said, "and I'll give your flesh to the birds of the air and the beasts of the field!"[48]

No translation necessary. No hidden messages. No ulterior motives.

Losers look down on others.

God's Giants

David looked his enemy in the eye.

He said, "You come at me with sword and spear and javelin, but I come against you in the name of the Lord. Today, I'll defeat you so the whole world will know there is a God."

God's giant knows victory belongs to the Lord.

Goliath fought from the standpoint of advantage, and David from disadvantage.

To Goliath, size mattered. To the giant, heart is what counts.

Goliath covered himself in armor. The giant covered himself in prayer.

Goliath was an individual superstar. The giant fought as part of a team, something greater than himself.

Goliath believed it was a one-on-one match. The giant believed God determines who is champion.

David picked up a stone and put it in his sling. He slung it round and round and let go, striking Goliath right where he aimed, right in the eye. The stone sank into Goliath's head and he fell. David then took Goliath's own sword and cut off Goliath's head.

David triumphed. He was God's giant.
- He ignored every message of failure.
- He defeated every messenger of bad news.
- He believed he belonged in battle.
- He believed, with God, he was more than able.
- He believed that victory belongs to the Lord.

In life, God's giants always get ahead.

Chapter 9

The Prodigal Father

"I wish you were dead!"

It wasn't exactly a Father's Day message, but they were exactly the words he meant to say.

And the father knew it. The father had experienced plenty of his son's attitude.

Oh, the son wasn't stupid. He said it in different words and perhaps a different tone. He didn't say everything he was thinking. But the demand was the same.

"Give me my inheritance, my portion of your estate. I wish you were dead so I could get all your blessings. I wish you were gone so everything you've worked for and saved all your life would be mine right now. I can't wait. You're just in the way. You're interfering with my fun and my life."

After all, what is an estate but the assets of a deceased person?

Perfect Father, Prodigal Son

He must have been around sixteen years "bold."

He'd learned enough of life. He no longer needed wisdom from his father. He had all the answers. The common disease called "eighteen-itis" hit him early. There is generally only one cure. He would not get better until he had to pay his own bills.

However, the son wasn't ready to pay bills; he was ready to party. He couldn't wait. His time had come.

Isn't that where most people are: looking for the party?

Unfortunately, people like the son don't always see the fun and blessings of home. And church? Who gives two cents for religion that is boring and empty?

For all the good reasons to go to church, it still all boils down to this: We are all looking for the party.

But it's a different kind of party, one with deep fellowship and friendship, abundant laughter and love, a meaningful purpose in life. Find all that, and we've found a real party. A real life!

That's what great worship is! Worship is where we are built up and feel like we just crashed a great party. We are alive!

Jesus taught that the father in this story represents our perfect Heavenly Father.

So even with perfect fathers, perfect families and churches, sons can still be prodigal and choose the wrong party.

Prodigal Papa

Most fathers would say, "Look, Bucko, I don't care how old you are.

I'm not about to let you go off and squander my wealth on wild living. I'm not going to enable you. What kind of father would I be if I gave you all my greatest blessings before you're ready? No, you are not prepared to receive my greatest blessings.

I'll show you the door, and you won't get one penny. You can just hit the road empty-handed if that's what you want. You'll have to learn the hard way."

No one would blame such a father. But this father was different. He gave and gave and gave some more. He gave his pride, his dreams, and his wealth. He simply divided up his property and gave it to the son.

If any strings were attached, we don't know about them.

No argument. No last-minute lectures.

Whatever their history of disagreements might be, they didn't rehash it. After all, it's simply too late to start training a child when his mind is made up a few days before he leaves home.

The giving was peaceful and generous and without reservation because the father was prodigal.

The story traditionally known as "The Prodigal Son,"[49] should have been named "The Prodigal Father."

It was the father who was lavish, wasteful, extravagant, excessive, and unrestrained.

Because of love, the papa was prodigal.

Paying for the Party

Demanding what he did not deserve, the son received his inheritance.

The Prodigal Father

Trusting what was in his pocket he left home and went out to take on the world. He partied at the father's expense. He went to Las Vegas. He gambled, drank, and had a wild time.

Then, much sooner than expected, the enormous amount of money was gone. In one short Bible verse, the son found the party, partied hard, and it was over.[50]

Now that's a lesson in itself. He squandered his wealth in wild living and spent everything. Just like that, he was broke. Busted.

His friends fled. There were tabs to pick up, bills to pay. It was time to get a job.

That's the problem with most parties. They end. They're over in an hour or two.

Then what? A hangover, a migraine, a stomachache, a visit to the doctor!

Then what? Sexually transmitted disease, an unplanned pregnancy, medical bills, dashed dreams, brokenness, poverty.

Then where are we? The hospital, the unemployment line, a strange country, out on the streets!

If we find the wrong party, we go nowhere fast. We go down instead of up. We go backward, not forward.

Everyone eventually finds a party, but if it's the wrong party, it soon ends, and there are always consequences to pay.

Stinkin' and Starvin'

After the son spent everything, there was a severe famine in that country, and he was in serious need.

He asked a citizen of that country for a job, and he was sent to the fields to feed pigs. He longed to fill his stomach with the pods that the pigs were eating, but no one gave him anything.

That's what happens when we look for the party in all the wrong places. We find what we are looking for but end up—down. Then we look up from the mud and think, "That stinking pig slop sure does look good right now.

Excuse me, Mr. Pig, that corncob you gnawed on and snorted to the side has a couple of kernels left on it. Mind if I dust it off?"

But as low as he was, it could have been worse. No matter how bad life is, our own wrong choices can always make it worse. We complain, only to dig our hole deeper. Discontentment leads us farther into debt. If we don't wake up, we may have that mental breakdown or heart attack.

In the end no one will give us anything—no one but the prodigal father.

Slaves and Stars

Those who look for the party in drugs should know one thing for sure: in the end, the dealers don't care about anyone but themselves.

The drug industry is a devil's trap. Ultimately, it enslaves all who give them money. Warlords and terrorists who seek to destroy the American way of life end up with the profits.

They own and enslave the people who pay them.

Those who search for a party in music that promotes sex and violence will reap the same loss of freedom. The idolized rock star with a life-sized poster in the kid's bedroom can put chains on children. He or she distorts good values.

Many celebrities gradually destroy themselves as well as the kids who listen to their music. Some in the music industry need children's money, for their own rehabilitation in drug treatment centers.

Young people don't see the connection between the music they listen to and their own personal troubles. They are blind to the link between the cost of their music and their inability to pay rent. They can afford CDs, but they miss the car payment. Their priorities are a mess, their character destroyed.

No matter how much a girl supports a pop star financially or personally, the celebrity will not return the favor. No matter how much a boy says they love that idol, once he is broke and broken, once enslaved, the famous star will not give him anything in return.

But the prodigal father will.

Lavish Love

The son came to his senses.

He said to himself, "How many of my father's hired men have plenty of food to spare? And here I am, starving to death! I will get up and go back home. I'll say, 'Father, I have sinned against heaven and against you. I am no longer worthy to be called your son. Make me like one of your hired men.'"

So he got up and went to his father.

What does a prodigal father do?

First, he gives and gives and gives when it might not always look smart.

Second, he loves and loves and loves.

While the son was still a long way from home, his father saw him and was filled with compassion for him. He ran to his son, threw his arms around him, and kissed him.

He called to his servant, "Quick! Bring the best robe and put it on him. Put a ring on his finger and sandals on his feet. Let's grill some steaks! Let's have a feast and celebrate! Let's party! For this son of mine was dead and is alive again; he was lost and now he is found."

In prodigal fashion, the father is not afraid to waste love, to lavishly pour it out, to spill it recklessly all over the place, and to be irresponsibly overgenerous and excessively unrestrained in love.

Supplies with Smiles

Talk about prodigal!

Most fathers would see him coming, sit down on the front porch rocking chair, and prepare a quick three-point lecture.

An assortment of opening lines would be considered:

"I told you so."

"Have you learned your lesson?"

"Care to eat any crow for supper?"

But that's not the prodigal father. He's filled to overflowing with compassion. No matter what we've done, our Heavenly Father eagerly runs to us, throws His arms wide open and tells us He loves us. He doesn't hesitate to forgive. He's not reluctant. He doesn't ask a hundred questions first to see if we are worthy.

We don't deserve anything, but He immediately throws a party.

The real blessing wasn't the inheritance. The blessing was the prodigal father himself. In his relationship with his father, the son had access to everything his father owned. When he partied at his father's house, he had everything he needed. There was no shortage of supplies.

Back with the prodigal father, the son once again had it all.

And the father was happy.

Doorway Distance

Out in the field, the older son heard music.

From the direction of the house, the sound of music and laughter filled the air. The hard-working son headed home to check it out.

He asked one of the servants, "What is going on?"

The servant explained that his wild young brother had come home, and the family was celebrating.

The older son was furious. He refused to step foot in the house. He wouldn't join the party. He wouldn't even watch.

Misery is watching as those we won't forgive have a good time. Jealousy and anger toward a brother or sister separates far too many families.

But the prodigal father is not restrained by our perceptions of fairness and equality. He's more than fair.

He's good. He gives us a choice. He invites us in where he is to be happy and celebrate what is not deserved.

We may not travel to a distant land. We may not go far at all. We may not do any of the rash things the son did. We may even stay just outside the door of the church.

But just outside the door, we can be as separated from the father as if we had traveled to a distant country.

Party of Prodigals

Everything the prodigal father has belongs to his children, even those who return and are undeserving!

If you've never had an earthly father who provides well and is prodigal in his blessings, it's hard to relate.

If you've been abandoned or abused by your father, this one is not an easy lesson to understand. A negative earthly father can prevent us from understanding our perfect and prodigal Heavenly Father.

To get past our problems and have the best life possible, we must have a relationship with our prodigal Heavenly Father. With Him, our blessings are abundant and endless.

Our perfect Heavenly Father is there for us, specifically because no one has a perfect earthly father.

Our Heavenly Father, though, is perfect, prodigal, just for you and me.

Earthly fathers and human brothers often become excuses for avoiding a relationship with our prodigal Heavenly Father. As a result, blessings and happiness are lost.

Today is a good day to improve relationships. You don't have to say much. Just show up. Be together. Make that phone call. Write that note. Express thanks.

Time is short. Opportunities pass quickly.

Forgiveness is the doorway.

Forgive your earthly father. He's prodigal.

Forgive your earthly brother. He's prodigal.

And do yourself a favor: forgive your Heavenly Father. He's perfect, so there is really nothing to forgive, but He's prodigal. Get used to it.

What about you? Don't exempt yourself. You're prodigal too.[51]

Only prodigals are allowed at this party.

Our prodigal Father came to earth. He left the party in heaven to come to where we stand. He invites us to come in to the great party with His son Jesus.

He begs us to choose joy. Come in and be the happy one.

Experience his lavish, wasteful, extravagant, excessive, overgenerous, and unrestrained love.

Chapter 10

"Tell 'Em Who Your Daddy Is!"

She was only fifteen, but she won the title of the most beautiful girl in the world.

She was winner of the Miss Universe pageant.

Of all the lovely girls from across the land, she was an ideal champion, chosen by the most powerful king on earth.

She would become his queen—like it or not.

Learning to Love

The young queen-to-be did not really know the king.

She knew only of him. She was not an insider. She was nominated to enter the pageant by community folks, acquaintances, and the king's men, but they knew her only on the surface.

She did not fill out the usual application with her first, middle, and last name. She listed no home address. She did

"Tell 'Em Who Your Daddy Is!"

not sign the fine print at the bottom stating her agreement with the conditions and terms of her prize winnings.

The king therefore, did not really know his chosen queen.

He chose her only for her outward beauty in a long line-up of model women. Perhaps she competed in a talent contest. She may have had a personality profile. But in making his final selection, the king did not know her.

Family background mattered little. After all, the king was open-minded and modern. He planned to get to know her.

No thought was given with regard to the custom of asking the father for the girl's hand in marriage. It didn't matter to the king who the father was. All that mattered to him was the girl's ability to learn her role as queen. If she failed, she would be replaced.

Her feelings? The king believed that any reasonable girl would be happy to become his queen.

Did she love him? Certainly not!

Could she learn to love him? How could she know?

From Peasant to Palace

Before receiving her crown, the girl enrolled for a year in the royal beauty school.

Living next door to the palace, she received all the treatments and training that money could buy. After all, she was unprepared for royalty. Even the King of Persia knew that a queen requires more than outward beauty. She must learn how to respect the king. She must display inner strength and wisdom.

The girl had a lot to learn, for she had lived the poor, common life of a peasant. Her upbringing was far removed from high society or any knowledge of social graces.

But when she won the king's favor, she suddenly found herself living in the palace.

Orphaned and Adopted

It all began in the land of Is Real, when Esther was born.

Her parents, family, and relatives were captured and deported to live as slaves in a foreign country, a country considered the greatest on earth. There, while she was just a little girl, her parents died.

Esther was then placed in foster care with her cousin, Mordecai. He raised her in a single-parent home. Eventually, Mordecai became her adopted father, and he cared for her as if she were his own daughter.

In spite of her background of being from a broken family, in spite of her early childhood instability and trauma, God blessed her with a parent who wanted the very best for her.

Strategy of Secrecy

He was a single parent.

It's one thing to be raised by a single parent, but a single parent who is a man?

That does not fit the norms of any society. Children should be raised by women. Ideally, they should have a mother and a father.

No wonder Mordecai taught her early in life not to discuss her family background. He trained Esther to keep their family story a secret. She would have far less trouble growing up in a foreign land if she kept quiet.

"Don't ever tell 'em who your daddy is," Mordecai advised.

A strategy of secrecy would help them stay together. People who objected to their living situation would not remove her from his care.

"Don't ever discuss me as your adopted father. Don't explain to anyone you are from the land of Is Real. If people know the real you, it will only cause problems. And above all, don't ever tell anyone who your Heavenly Father is."

Messages from Mordecai

After Esther won the king's favor in the beauty pageant, Mordecai moved near the palace.

He stayed just outside the palace gate, waiting for hours to see across the courtyard and perhaps talk to Esther. He found ways to send her messages.

Mordecai was concerned about his adopted daughter. He didn't just walk away and say, "I have her raised now, and she has all the wealth she needs to be happy. I've done my good deed. She'd better make the best of a fine situation."

Mordecai knew that children don't really grow up overnight. He wanted to know how she was doing. It was a good thing he showed concern.

Sitting near the palace gate, Mordecai overheard two government officials whispering together. They were gatekeepers to the inner and outer courts. Angry with the king, they plotted his assassination.

Mordecai sent a message to Esther, and she revealed their evil intent to the king. The wicked men were captured and killed. The king was very pleased with Esther for saving his life, but she did not take credit. She told the king that his life was saved because of Mordecai.[52]

In all this, Esther remembered her agreement never to identify her father.

Power Play

A second secret emerged at this time.

Another crafty man sought an opportunity against the king. The king's highest-ranking officer, Haman, dreamed of becoming the next king. So strong was his desire that he may have been in on the previous conspiracy to murder the king.

Haman held unmatched authority and position among government officials, but it wasn't enough.

Haman wanted more; he wanted someday to become the most powerful man in the world. He abused his position. He commanded all the people to bow down to him when he was in their presence.

Everywhere he went with his government escort, Haman demanded to be treated as royalty.

When the king wasn't looking, he pretended to be all-powerful.

Last Laugh

One person in all the land refused to bow down to Haman: Mordecai.

This made Haman furious. He became obsessed with Mordecai, who was nothing more than a slave from the land of Is Real. Unable to gain complete control of this one person, Haman became consumed with hatred.

Haman had power and prestige that was second only to the king. Millions of people bowed to him, yet all Haman could think about was one person who would not bend his knee. Haman had it all, but he was deeply disturbed. He had no happiness, so he had nothing. Unhappy Haman!

Eaten up by one person and one thought, Haman decided to punish Mordecai. Like an evil dictator, like a king who wants to be a god, Haman planned to prove his power to Mordecai and everyone else. He would not tolerate any refusal to bow to him.

Haman ordered a gallows built seventy-five feet high on which he planned to hang Mordecai for the whole land to see. He would make an example of Mordecai. No one would ever mess with Haman again.

In addition, Haman announced that he would exterminate all of Mordecai's people within the year. If they were the kind who would not bend their knees, if they believed a Heavenly Father was their King, then they would be annihilated.

Mordecai might not bow for his own sake, but Haman believed he would bow before he watched his whole nation wiped out.

He would have the pleasure of watching Mordecai beg for his life and for the people of Is Real. Then he would bow.

The last laugh would be Haman's.

Honor and Hate

Back at the palace, the king knew nothing of Haman's abuse of power, but he must have sensed trouble because he couldn't sleep well.

Once, in the middle of the night, he asked to have his history read so he could hear what others would hear if he were dead. He wanted to experience the record of his life, to be soothed by his success. After all, he had done great things. He had championed many causes for the people.

As the history was narrated, the king was reminded of how Mordecai had saved his life. He wished more people were model citizens like Mordecai.

"Anyone who saved the king," he thought, "should be greatly rewarded!"

The next morning, Haman approached the king to ask that Mordecai be hung on the gallows, but the king first asked Haman, "What should be done for the man who has greatly pleased the king?"

Haman was so egotistical that he thought the king was talking about honoring him.

Haman said, "The man who pleases the king should be publicly recognized. He should be paraded through the land on the king's own horse. He should wear the king's own robe. The horse should be led by the king's noblest prince. The prince should loudly and repeatedly announce to all the people, "This man has most greatly pleased the king!"

The king said, "Very well, Haman! You put the king's robe on Mordecai. Lead Mordecai on the king's horse throughout the land and make your announcement. Do not fail to do everything you have just recommended."

At the end of that day, Haman went home dejected and humiliated.[53] The man he hated and despised was the very man he had spent the whole day honoring.

It bought Mordecai some time, but it only made Haman hate him more.

A Saving Secret

Esther looked out her window.

The gallows towered into the air above the rooflines. They were built to hang her adoptive father, Mordecai.

But there was more news out on the street. Word was that Haman had promised to wipe out all the people from Is Real. Esther's people were in mourning. They were preparing their own funerals. Time was running out. They faced a holocaust.

Esther was greatly distressed. Everyone knew Haman could deceive the king and get away with it.

Esther thought of talking to the king, but there were three problems.

First, with his attention confined to his troubles, the king was out of touch. Queen Esther had not been called to visit him in the last thirty days.

Second, the law restricted anyone, including the queen, from approaching the king unless he called for them first. His reputation demanded respect, and this was required especially from the queen! He had had enough disrespect from the previous queen.[54] Esther would approach the king now at her own risk, even the risk of death.

Third, what would she say if she couldn't tell her secret?

She needed to tell the king that her first father was from the land of Is Real, that her adoptive father was Mordecai, and that she believed, along with all of her people, that she had a Heavenly Father.

But she had promised never to identify her real daddy.

She thought deeply. Was it wise to save a secret?

Or was the secret itself in reality a saving secret?

Love or Law

Mordecai counseled Esther, saying, "Esther, this is not just about me, and it's not only about our family. It's about you, too.

"Don't think that you will be spared if all the people from Is Real are killed. Don't even think of saving yourself. You can't continue to keep your secret from the king. It's time to tell your secret. You are from Is Real. The truth always comes out! I release you from your promise. You must now appeal to the king. Tell him who your father is! Tell him everything!"

Then Mordecai said these famous words. "Who knows, Esther; perhaps you have been raised to live in the palace for just such a time as this!"

Strong words! Words of faith! Words on which to build courage!

A thread of hope hung on through the fear. Her whole life would be meaningless if she did not act in faith!

Faith says, "I have a purpose!" Fear says, "I am in peril."

Faith says, "I'm in the perfect position!" Fear says, "I'm in a predicament."

Faith says, "I can save others!" Fear says, "I must save myself."

Esther fasted and prayed. She asked Mordecai and the people to do the same. At the end of three days, she said, "If I must die, I am willing."

Because of love, she decided to risk her life and approach the king even though it violated the law.

Boasting and Bragging

When Esther approached the king, his love for her was stronger than any law he had made.

He welcomed her and held out his gold scepter as a gesture of acceptance. He said, "Esther, what do you want? Ask for anything, and it will be given."

Whew!

Esther was ready. She had hoped for the best! She said, "I want the king and your officer, Haman, to come to a banquet I'm preparing for you tomorrow. Then I will tell you what I want."

The king agreed.

When Haman received his invitation to the banquet, he was full of himself. He told his wife and friends that, of all the people in the kingdom, he alone was invited to dinner with the king and queen. Haman boasted of his great wealth.

He bragged how the king had honored and promoted him above all the other officials and leaders.

Beware What You Build

Then Haman looked out of his window and saw Mordecai.

Sitting at the gate was the man who refused to stand up in Haman's presence, the man who would not bow to him, and the man who would not beg for Haman's mercy.

Haman planned to take advantage of Esther's banquet the next day. After all, only the three most important people in the world would be there. He would ask the king to hang Mordecai on the gallows immediately.

At dinner the next day, before Haman could ask for anything, the king asked Esther what she wanted.

She then revealed her secret: her birth father, her adopted father, her Heavenly Father.

Esther broke down and begged mercy from the king to have her life and the lives of all who were being prepared for holocaust spared.

The king asked, "What are you talking about? Why ask me to spare your life?"

Esther replied, "An evil enemy has marked my people and me for destruction, slaughter, and annihilation."

"Who could this enemy possibly be?" the king asked.

Pointing her finger, Esther said, "This wicked Haman has ordered it to be so. He is our adversary! He is the enemy of my earthly father, my adopted father, and my Heavenly Father!"

Immediately, the King had Haman arrested and hung on the very gallows he had built for Mordecai.

In pursuit of power, beware what you build.

Promised Promotion

Mordecai was promoted to the highest rank in the kingdom.

The royal signet ring was reclaimed from Haman's finger and placed on Mordecai's.

Holocaust averted! Human rights restored!

The people of Is Real feasted and celebrated as never before. Joy ruled the land.

Mordecai became the much-loved adoptive father of a whole nation, but the real heroine was a beautiful, brave, orphaned, adopted teenager, Queen Esther.

Many years later, Jesus summed up a similar lesson: "If you want to be saved, you can't keep it a secret! You will have to confess the name of your Heavenly Father."[55]

You'll have to tell 'em who your real daddy is!

Chapter 11

Life after Juvey

A jailhouse is a hard place for a boy to grow into a man.
It was especially hard for J.J., a convicted rapist serving a long term behind bars.

A repeat offender, he had spent half his life in prison.

His background fit the usual profile of a prisoner.

J.J. came from a broken home.

Tattletale

Like his dad, J.J. had poor social skills and great difficulty relating to people.

His dad had been married four times. Each of the marriages was a rocky, unstable relationship. His dad was notorious for going back and forth between the women in his life. In all, his dad had fathered fourteen children—perhaps more he didn't know about.

It was a rough family. Two of his brothers had been convicted of armed robbery and murder.

The siblings were mean to J.J. They nicknamed him T.T. just to torment him, but he was no angel; he brought a lot of it on himself.

J.J. thought he was close to his family, but none of them ever wrote or visited him while he was in prison.

He was locked up for the first time when he was a teenager. Soon after his release, his family shipped him off to a big city and said, "You're on your own." They broke all ties, and J.J. eventually lost contact with them.

With an incomplete education, the first thing J.J. did was find a minimum-wage job in a huge government industry. Fortunately, large numbers of employees were being hired. His boss was tough, and J.J. spent his earnings on his room and board in the company-supplied housing. He was going nowhere fast, a slave to "the system."

Eventually, J.J. earned a promotion, and it looked like things might get better, but that was before the rape conviction of Jailhouse Joseph, better known to his brothers as "Tattle Tale."[56]

Time to Think

The first time he was incarcerated, he was in a pit in the ground, an empty cistern where his brothers intended to leave him for dead.

It was a juvenile jail for the hardest of criminals.

No cable TV. No bed. No food. No light. No legal services. No appeals.

By then, it was too late to take back all the bragging he had done to his brothers about how he would be the greatest, most successful person in his family. More than that, his brothers would someday all bow down to him.

He had dreamed it!

It was too late to undo the damage of his stupid strutting.

His father had favored him, giving him an expensive beautiful, multi-colored coat. The other boys did not get one. It made them angry at their father and their brother.

While the brothers fussed at J.J. about his dreams, Dad never did. He was uncomfortable in the family fuss, but he wouldn't hold his boy back. He pondered the situation and even found himself dreaming a little through his son.

It's no wonder his brothers hated him.[57] J.J. was such a dreamer.

The brothers decided to put a stop to J.J.'s dreams. A healthy dose of reality would end his fantasies once and for all. They stripped him of his coat and threw him into an old dried-up water well. They intended to leave him for dead.

J.J. could not stop their plans to kill him.

He found his own private death row a busy place to be because there was plenty of time to think.

From Pit to Prosperity

It took a deep, dark pit for J.J. to see clearly.

He had caused some of their hatred.

The only ray of light he saw was when he looked up. It's never too late to change heart, although that is something many people never accomplish.

J.J. prayed at the bottom of a well just like Jonah prayed in the belly of a whale.

His brothers saw a chance to make some money. Thinking they would never have to deal with J.J. again, they sold him into slavery and sent him off to Egypt.

It's strange how prayers are answered at times! At least he wasn't dead! J.J. had lost his coat, but he still had his dream!

In Egypt, J.J. worked for Potiphar, a high-ranking military commander.

"And the Lord prospered Joseph, blessed him, and gave him success in everything he did."[58]

Little Things, Big Difference

Potiphar noticed something special about Jailhouse Joseph.

He had one of the secret ingredients for success: J.J. could be trusted to do the right thing!

Success is a strange word in the context of slavery. We could understand a successful manager or a successful supervisor, but a successful slave?

Like J.J., we dream of inheriting the top position.
We want to start out as manager. We apply for the job of supervising. We don't want to start at the bottom. We want instant success. Our climb up the ladder starts on step four out of five.

But success doesn't come that way.

Jesus gave this principle for success: "When we are faithful in a few little things, we will be put in charge of bigger things."[59]

Success is found in small steps for those who are willing to work, who will start at the bottom and build a foundation for the future. Success as a slave is a valid concept for making it to the top.

Many object, saying, "I don't see how all these little things—chores, manners, tending my room, a math assignment—make a real difference in my life. When it comes to the big things, then I'll do my best."

Sorry, but that's not how life really works, not in the land of Is Real.

Unless you are faithful in little things, your opportunity for big things will never come. The successful person breaks big jobs down into small tasks that can be managed. Long-term success in marriage comes when we fan the flames of love with small favors, flowers, compliments, or holding hands. Little things add up to make a big difference.

J.J. did even the little things right, so Potiphar put him in charge of everything in his house and let him live in a wing of the palace. It was a tremendous responsibility and position, but Potiphar knew this employee would not break trust.

Then he gave Joseph a brand new coat.

Sacred Secret

Like any employer, Potiphar placed a high value on trust, but he couldn't trust everyone, including his own wife.

Day after day, she made secret advances toward J.J.

For a slave, it was great temptation. A relationship with a powerful woman might be a dream come true.

An affair with a rich woman could look like just what was needed: a lucky break.

J.J., however, refused to break trust. He saw that tricky ticket to freedom as a death trap. Most other slaves would have given her advances serious consideration. Perhaps if he cut some corners off his God-given principles, he could have a real future.

Secret agreements might change his situation. After all, God blessed J.J. with good looks. He could use the blessing as part of an exit strategy. If he was ever going to escape the system, he was going to have to find his own way. Reasonable, right?

Enough of this mundane existence! According to his God-given dreams, his destiny was greatness, not that of a common man.

But the temptation would be a killer in the end, and J.J. saw it. Two masters instead of one never make a person free—just more of a slave. Adultery is a home-wrecker. Marital affairs separate kids from parents. Secret encounters divide a house against itself. It never honors God when the oneness of marriage turns into divorce.

A secret to success in any endeavor, including building a solid marriage relationship, is being a person who will not break a sacred trust.

To find that kind of person to marry, we must be that kind of person.

No Nonsense

One day, Potiphar's wife cornered J.J. when he was alone.

Advancing forcefully, she pushed herself upon him until he ran from her. She grabbed his coat, but he slipped out and left it in her empty arms. Humiliated and angry, she accused J.J. of attempted rape and claimed that his new coat was evidence.

If Potiphar really believed his wife, he would have killed J.J. Instead, Potiphar saved face with his own household by throwing Joseph in the jailhouse to serve a life sentence.

It is not always immediately clear that resisting such advances as that J.J. received from Potiphar's wife will bring success. In this case, saying "no" landed Joseph in the jailhouse. But in the long run, saying "no" also saved his life and set the stage for the future.

Down before Up

For people at the top, success comes in the shape of a checkmark, as they go down before they go up.

In other words, they find a degree of failure before success.

In athletics, the success-shaped learning curve is the Nike "swoosh." Baseball professionals strike out many more times than they ever hit home runs. Michael Jordan was cut from his freshman basketball team.

They all learned to turn failure into success.

In marriage and family, producing successful children is the graph of a baby's heartbeat. Before most marriages can become fruitful, some problems must be worked out. Adjustments must be made. Parenting is full of trial and error.

For every Christian champion, the learning curve has a dip in it. The trip to the top starts by first moving to the bottom. Whoever would be exalted, must first be humbled.

The good news of the death, burial, and resurrection of Jesus charts a dip. It does not shoot straight to the top. It goes down before it goes up.

Choose to Be Champion

Joseph could have blamed his predicament on his father and his family, using those problems as an excuse to be bitter and mess up his life. Instead, he learned from his mistakes and made the best of his life.

One person with a drinking problem blames it on alcoholic parents, but a twin sister abstains and says, "I learned from my alcoholic parents. I'm sober because I don't want my family and children to have the same problems."

One person's excuse for failure is another's strategy for success. What we have been through can ruin us, or it can prepare us uniquely for what lies ahead.

We are never trapped. We can choose.

Jesus told Peter, "When you're old, they're going to take you where you don't want to go." He was referring to a jailhouse and, later, an execution.

Today, people often go where they don't want to go; some to a hospital, others to a rest home, a boot camp, a job, a children's home.

You may not be able to change where you are, but you can always choose your attitude. You can always choose to trust God and treat people right.

As a result, you can always choose to be happy.

Responsibility Rollercoaster

In prison, the warden noticed that J.J. had a second secret of success.

Not only would he do the right thing, he was also responsible in the way he treated people.

"The warden put Joseph in charge of all those held in prison, and he was made responsible for all that was done there. The warden paid no attention to anything under Joseph's care, because the Lord was with Joseph and gave him success in all he did."[60]

The same boy who began with broken family relationships and poor social skills was now good at managing people and winning friends. What appeared to be a demotion to the dungeon was in reality a promotion! It was preparation for what lay ahead.

It doesn't matter if you're moving from caretaker of a king's palace to managing the lowliest of people; if you are stepping into God's plan, it's a step up.

Why? Because people—even prisoners, and maybe especially prisoners—are more valuable than things.

People with problems are where the successful market their skills, services, and products to make life better. If we aspire to attain a higher level of excellence, if we dream of rising to the top, we must learn to deal with those who are difficult.

J.J. learned the Golden Rule: to treat people with respect, the way he wanted to be treated.

Dreams or Depression

In the jailhouse there were plenty of prisoners who were down and dejected.

J.J. noticed. He cared. He did what he could to help them be happy, even in prison.

Two inmates were having trouble sleeping. Night after night, they had strange nightmares, and they didn't know what they meant. J.J. asked them to tell him about their disturbing dreams. He told them, "The answer to all dreams is found in God!"[61]

It was an amazing statement of faith. After years of imprisonment, with no end in sight, J.J. still believed in God's faithful watch over his life.

He could have easily comforted his inmates with negative thoughts, saying something like "I understand how dreams can mess you guys up. When I was young, I was a dreamer, but my dreams never came true. My family disowned me. I've been falsely accused and imprisoned. Look where I ended up: forgotten, doing time in maximum security. There's no sense in even dreaming of escape or ever getting out. We have to accept our situation. Sometimes bad things just happen."

We can be imprisoned by our thinking.

Faith avoids the depression of man-made thinking, choosing the alternative of a far-fetched God-given dream. The only real prison is where no dreams are allowed. J.J. knew he had to dream with his fellow prisoners. When all looked hopeless, they had to leave room for God to work it all out. It would happen in God's time.

Dreams were all they had to hang on to, but a God-given dream is a solid stepping stone on which to climb up from the bottom. A God-given dream is the hope that will take the dreamer all the way to the top.

J.J. became the head prisoner/manager in the jailhouse, and with God's help, he interpreted the dreams of his inmates.

And he wore the same coat as everyone else.

I Can't, God Can

Pharoah, King of Egypt, had a nightmare.

It bothered him greatly. He could not get it out of his mind. It wouldn't go away.

Pharoah searched across the land for someone who could provide an answer for what the dream meant. His magicians and fortune tellers could not explain the meaning. Among all the wise men of Egypt, no one could help.

One day, Pharoah heard about a guy down in the prison, a guy nicknamed "Dreamer." It was a long shot, but Pharoah was desperate. He called the prison, asked for J.J., and said, "I've heard you interpret dreams."

J.J. answered, "I can't, but God can. The answer to all your dreams is in God."[62]

When Pharoah described his dream, J.J. explained that it was simple in meaning: "The world will encounter seven years of abundant crops and seven years of famine." He advised Pharoah to select the wisest man he could find to be in charge of collecting food for Egypt. Grain should be stored in abundance to prepare the people for the difficult years ahead.

Pharoah recognized J.J. as the only person who could interpret his dream, so he did exactly what Joseph advised: He appointed J.J. as governor of Egypt.

The Bible says Pharoah thought of J.J. so highly that he eventually revered him as a father. With that, J.J. became one of the most powerful people in the world.

And Pharoah gave him another new coat.

Dreamers or Beggars

For the next fourteen years, as governor, J.J. prospered.

He married and had a family of his own. When his first son was born, he said, "God has made me forget all my family troubles." When his second son was born, he said, "God has turned my suffering into success."[63]

That's good news. Family dreams come true!

No matter what your problems have been, God can make you forget your troubles and turn your suffering into success. He will bless you with a new family.

Your God-given dream includes your future family, your future spouse, and your future children. Your God-given dream includes all the love you ever thought possible.

J.J. was successful in storing food during the abundant years. When the famine followed, the whole world traveled to Egypt for food.

One day, his brothers walked in, asking for grain. Had they been dreamers, his brothers would have recognized J.J., but they didn't know him. Those who refuse to become dreamers become beggars.

They bowed to J.J.

J.J. realized that the God-given dream he had had as a boy, that they all would bow to him someday came true before his very eyes.

Family Forgiveness

J.J. was deeply moved.

He had grown past any childish desire to tell his brothers, "I told you so." He hurried into his private room and wept.

When he had collected himself, he went to his brothers, and with tears streaming down his face, he said, "It's me, J.J. Remember? The brother you threw in the pit and sold into slavery many years ago?"

They were so afraid, they could not answer him.

J.J. said, "Come close to me. Don't be afraid."

He threw his arms around them and kissed them all.

Life after Juvey

The brothers begged forgiveness and again threw themselves down, bowing before J.J..

"We are your slaves," they said.

It was the beginning of a new concept; success as a slave.

By then, in spite of his high position, J.J. had given up being in the place of God. He knew that life is not about getting what is deserved. He knew his dream wasn't meant to hurt his brothers, but to help them.

He said again, "Get up. Don't be afraid."

Then he blessed their lives with unforgettable words. These words are an important blessing for every person who aspires to become a Christian champion.

"You intended to harm me," J.J. said, "but everything you did to me and all that happened since then was part of God's plan. God used your plans for his own good purpose. This has all been God's plan for saving our family and the rest of the world. It wasn't really you who sent me away, then, but God."[64]

Only God makes dreams come true.

J.J. gave his brothers the best land and livestock in Egypt.

And he gave each brother a beautiful new coat.

Chapter 12

A Lot of Bull and a Baby

Three teenagers grew up way too fast.
   The first one left home before her parents were ready.
The second left her parents before she was ready.
The third was very young when his father died.

Soul Selling

The first girl had deep resentments.
   She grew up in a poor family and hated it. She blamed their lack of money for her parent's divorce. She never had enough, she thought; life hadn't been fair to her. She developed a deep, desperate desire for money.
   The second girl had enough money, but she never felt loved by her father. All her life, she watched her mother suffer with the same feelings. The material blessings were there, but her father was always gone. Even when he was home, he was disconnected. He worked all the time. More than anything else, the girl wanted to be loved.

The first girl ran away from her mother, broke all ties and burned all bridges. She eventually turned to prostitution.

The second girl left home and went out on the streets as well. She doubted her dad would even miss her.

Soon the two girls met and moved in together, splitting the bills and spreading the love.

Selling their souls, one for money, the other for love, you wouldn't think they were teenagers.

Tolerant Times

The way they acted and looked aged them quickly.

Just when they thought it could get no harder, it did. The men told them they loved them, but they didn't provide a family. The men told them they loved them, but they left them alone.

In a short time, both girls were pregnant.

Business came to a halt. The men and the money left. The girls had babies out of wedlock. Life was tougher than it had ever been.

Like so many others, the two teenaged girls faced raising kids as single parents. It was hard enough just taking care of themselves. Now they had to provide for babies.

Had they lived in earlier days, they would have had no chance of survival, but times were changing. People's attitudes were different. They were more tolerant now.

They didn't stone people or condemn them like they had before.

And for good reason!

Lots of Love

The third teenager, grew up with good, Godly parents.

He never lacked for love or money. They were a wealthy family, and his parents expressed their deep love for him.

But his family had more than their share of problems. Beginning when he was only a boy, he heard rumors about his parents. He heard the stories the street people told, and he heard the revised versions. He didn't believe them until he was old enough, when he realized the rumors were true:

His own parents had conceived a child before marriage.

His father was looking for love, his mother for money!

The whole land of Is Real knew it.

Many people doubted that these new days of tolerance were best for raising kids, but they couldn't oppose the higher powers. Society had changed.

Before he could understand all he was hearing, his father died. The boy became fatherless at an early age, and he was raised in a single-parent home.

He developed a heart for children born out of wedlock, so when he inherited the throne from his father, he had much in common with the two teenage prostitutes.

Lots of money, lots of love.

Global Governing

Solomon was taught to love God.

He wanted to follow in his famous father's footsteps with a religious passion. His father's dying words to him were "Obey your God and follow His ways so you will be successful in all you do."

But it didn't go as well as David instructed. Even a boy who inherits a kingdom needs a father. Without David to raise and teach him, the boy missed much in his understanding.

As a boy king, Solomon offered a thousand burnt offerings, sacrifices on an altar to the gods.[65] Like a forest fire at the top of Mt. Gibeon, the smoke rose for miles around the country and into the distant lands. All the people heard about the famous boy king, but young Solomon did not have his head on straight. His day spent observing the slaughter of a thousand bulls was a mistake.

In Solomon's thinking, God was great, but tolerance, according to politically correct folks, meant there were 999 other gods. Solomon thought it best to please everyone. He'd cover all the bases and offend no one. That's how you invoke the maximum number of blessings and get lots of love and lots of money.

The boy king tried to appease everyone's gods, 999 of them—Confucious, Allah, Buddha, Indian gods, mountain gods, river gods, gods of money, fame, work, and pleasure, the oceans and stars, the sun and moon and more—and hundreds of religious isms of faith: New Age, Judaism, Legalism, Hinduism, Atheism, Agnosticism, Alcoholism, Addictionism.;

Standing on top of the mountain, the boy king saw a big world. He needed to engage in superior thinking. He might not believe in idolatry, but there were other viewpoints.

He knew he would have to govern globally.

That's why, as a boy, he married the daughter of Pharoah, King of Egypt.

Father Figure

Like so many people today, Solomon thought he had no problem with idolatry.

He neither made them nor worshiped them. He didn't carry a single idol to the top of Mt. Gibeon.

But he did herd 999 extra bulls up the mountain.

That's a lot of extra bull!

The first commandment is "You shall have no other gods before or besides me." Worship only the one true and living God. Reject all others. Pick a side, any side! No other gods on any sides. No gods before, beside, over, under, or around.

Whose side are you on, Solomon?

At the end of the day, the boy felt good about himself and his higher thinking at the high places. Having satisfied every possible god he could imagine, he laid down his head for a good night's rest. But he wrestled in his sleep. He faced all that responsibility.

In his dreams, one of the thousand gods Solomon had called upon spoke to him.

The other 999 slept.

"Solomon, ask for whatever you want me to give you."

Even though Solomon was all mixed up as a boy king, the one true and living God came to him. He knew the boy needed a father figure.

The Heavenly Father offered him a reward: "whatever you want!"

Before, Above and Beside

It was an act of mercy and love.

Our Heavenly Father's kindness is meant to lead us to Him as the only God. "If any would draw near to the Lord, he must first believe that he exists and rewards those who earnestly seek him."[66]

Solomon answered in the night, "I'm just a kid. I don't know what I'm doing. This job is too great. I need help. Give me Your wisdom."[67]

The Lord was pleased.

Solomon would receive all the other blessings that come from getting wisdom. Get wisdom first, and you get it all!

The next morning, Solomon returned to Jerusalem. The first thing he did was to offer many sacrifices and offerings. Perhaps he offered 999.

But this time, every bull was offered at the ark of the Lord, to the one Lord who spoke to him in the night. God's kindness caused Solomon to honor God and only God.

Solomon was excited about all the blessings and promises he had dreamed about. He threw a big party and held a feast for all his court. He was sending a new message to clear up any doubts.

They would all know that he recognized one God before, above, and besides all others.

Winning With Wisdom

One day, two girls in dispute came to stand before Solomon. They carried a baby.

One girl said, "My girlfriend and I live in the same house, all alone. Her baby son died because she lay on him one night. In distress, she came and took my baby son while I slept. She put her dead son in place of mine."

The other girl interrupted, "That's not true. The living one is mine."

They argued back and forth.

The boy king said, "Silence! Bring me a sword!"

The boy king gave an order that made everyone think he did not know what he was doing. "Cut the child in two, and give half to one and half to the other."

One of the girls begged, "Please don't kill him! Give the child to her!"

The other girl said, "Neither of us should have him. Cut him in two!"

The king then ordered, "Give the baby to the first woman. She is his mother."

The story spread across the land of Is Real, and the boy king was held in awe. Even in his youth, even though he was considered only half a man, he had wisdom from a Heavenly Father. He had wisdom beyond his years. The wisdom of a king!

Wisdom to be like his dad, a champion!

Chapter 13

Chances with the Champion

The gospels are full of stories of children and Jesus. They proclaim the Good News that Jesus loves children of all ages, classes, nationalities, and genders.

The gospel writers shared the story of Jesus' childhood and told at least sixteen stories about children. The examples teach how Jesus, as an adult, viewed the youth around him. Other examples show how he viewed other adults' attitudes toward youth.

Five of the stories were repeated, indicating their importance.

Each gospel writer shed a different light on the relationship Jesus had with children.

Each child had an encounter with Christ that transformed them him or her into a champion.

Plans Made Plain

Adults often do not understand God's plan for a particular child.

For many years they search for answers. A child may be completely grown and out of the house before any kind of sense can be made of God's greater purpose.

Parents and grandparents may ask for twenty years, "Why, God? Why is this child like this? It seems a bit more is needed here and there. You didn't quite make him complete. It appears a little something was left out of the recipe."

That was certainly true of the man in John 9.

He was born blind. He lived without sight for a long time, but His suffering wasn't meaningless. His parent's efforts were not worthless. God's purpose from the beginning was leading to an encounter with Christ. That's when the power of God came into the man's life.

God's plan is understandable once it comes to fruition. We wait upon the Lord, and at the right time, God's work is plain to see.

The Challenge of Children

Imagine their heartbreak when the parents first heard their baby was blind.

The nights became longer than normal. The days of yearning for the child to be able to take care of himself just a little never ended. Just learning to tie a shoe or put on clothes was twice as difficult as it should have been.

The early developmental years were prolonged. The parents adjusted their work schedules, giving up time at the office to help their son. The family bank account suffered.

With few resources, the blind boy grew to become just what the community expected: a couch potato, a beggar, another victim, another dependent.

Life is hard enough for the best of families in the best of situations. How much harder is it for those who have children with developmental delays?

But that wasn't the worst part of the child's handicap, at least not for the parents. Questions like "Who sinned, the child or the parents, that he was born blind?" from their social connections and "friends" hurt deeply.

The same question was asked in a hundred other variations. Oh, they were phrased differently, packaged nicely; but all were the same question. Who is to blame? What did you do wrong? Did you eat right? Did you take care of yourself? Why is God punishing you?

The community leaders could appear so friendly at times, but they sized up this handicapped family as a bunch of losers.

Jesus challenged their thinking. He astounded the greatest of religious minds. He answered boldly!

"You're not even asking the right question, and your multiple choices don't include the right answer: None of the above! Neither this man nor his parents sinned! This happened so the power of God might be displayed in his life."

Heaven's Handicap

Others might not have seen it, but Jesus saw this family as special, the very ones whom God would use in a mighty way.

The family had a lot going for it. They stayed together. They "hung in there" from the time the boy was born until well into his adult years. The parents had been responsible far beyond others with healthy children. They rallied around the child. They built their whole lives upon providing for his care.

Somehow, in their suffering, in doing the right thing every day, they became a close-knit family. There they are in the story, right there, always there, ready to take him down to the pool at a moment's notice.

Not so for the family down the street whose children were healthy enough. The parents both worked to make ends meet. Nothing detrimental affected their abilities in the workplace. Nothing held their children back in school. They seemed to have it all together. No apparent handicaps inflicted their souls in the beginning. There were relatively few sleepless nights. They didn't have to depend on each other as much, and they saw little need to depend on God.

But the family who had everything going for them grew apart. Divorce wrecked their home. They went separate ways. The children who had everything were into drugs. Addictions destroyed their lives and held them with demonic power.

Ah, yes! Among all the curses of life, a handicapped child is not one of them. Handicapped children can be the greatest of blessings from God!

Sixth Sense

When Jesus made new eyes for the blind man, he reminds us of the lady in the kitchen who knows her work so well that she doesn't need to go back to the recipe box. She uses a pinch here and a dab there.

God wasn't making a whole new body; He was making a body whole.

Taking a little dirt and a small part of himself, he had all the ingredients needed for a new pair of eyes. He spit in the dirt and made some mud. He smeared it in the eye sockets of the blind man.

The man could have been offended. Two top ways to insult people are to spit on them and to throw dirt on them.

Okay, Jesus, would you like to consider changing your approach? A bit rude and crude don't you think?

Years of suffering as a child could have made the handicapped man bitter. He could have said, "Hey, Mr. Light of the World, I don't care if You are the president. What's the big idea of messing with my eyes? I may be handicapped, but You cannot spit on me!"

But there was none of that. The blind man did not react like a normal person. Faith is not normal. Faith reacts differently. It's not touchy. It rolls with the punches.

As a child, the blind man had learned not to look for the bad. When people encountered him, he looked for the good.

Faith does not need sight. Sight needs faith!

Faith always develops a sixth sense.

The blind man had good sense. He knew he was in the presence of Someone good when Jesus came near.

Favored by Faith

The blind man did not know who put mud on him and told him to wash.

He didn't know who Jesus was until introductions were made after the healing. His faith was clear only when he courageously stood up to his critics in defense of Jesus.

Before the healing, Jesus saw that the blind man had the raw ingredients. He had what it took. He had kept his child-like faith. He didn't leave his child-like faith behind when he became an adult.

There is no indication of great faith. Maybe he had only the smallest faith, like that of a mustard seed. His faith may have been miniscule, but there was one thing great about his faith: the blind man followed Jesus instructions.

He knew what dirt felt like and knew he had been dirtied. He recognized his need and washed in the pool.

Obedience is a sign of faith.

So why did Jesus make mud and put it in the blind man's eyes? Why tell him to go wash in the pool?

Don't look too hard for a deep, difficult answer. Don't look for something spooky. It may be so simple we miss it!

He put mud in the man's eyes simply so he would know he needed to be washed!

And when he washed, he saw for the first time in his life!

Trust through Troubles

Jairus was the ruler of a synagogue.

He worked in something like a church and was like its pastor or preacher. Like many today, Jairus doubled as the janitor and groundskeeper. No task was too menial. He was willing to do whatever it took to keep the little church going. He prepared for the worship services and communion. He lined up the song leaders and preachers.

What a great guy, this Jairus! But Jairus had a daughter who died at twelve years old. That is a lesson in itself.

The position and job we hold is no free ticket into the easy life. Our willingness to serve the Lord does not exempt us from the need to trust Him with all the great difficulties common to man. No matter how dedicated we seem in our choice of employment, we must trust the Lord.

Troubles will come.

Frantic Faith

Shortly before his daughter died, Jairus began to realize just how sick his daughter was.

In a panic, he ran to the man he had heard could heal, a man off limits to synagogue rulers like Jairus.
The man did not keep the traditions. His reputation was not that of a law-keeping legalist. A relationship with Jesus was forbidden by the religious leaders.

That did not matter to Jairus, not now.

Jairus knew only that his daughter was close to death. The prohibitions of synagogue teachings and religion were suddenly worth nothing. They meant nothing if he could not help his daughter.

Normally, Jesus was on the far side of the lake, but when Jarius heard that Jesus' boat was on the way, Jairus ran to the shore. Panting and out of breath, Jairus threw himself at Jesus' feet, crying, "My little daughter is dying. Please come! Put Your hands on her so she will be healed and live."

An act of faith! Words of faith!

Jairus was not going to accept his daughter's death without a fight. He would do something—whatever it took!

No matter what he believed about Jesus, no matter what he had heard and been told, he knew that faith was important to God.

Traveling On Together

Before Jesus arrived at Jairus' home, the damage was done.

A couple of messengers met Jairus along the way and told him, "It's too late. Your daughter has died."

They urged Jairus to go and console his wife, the child's mother. Funeral arrangements needed to be made. There was much to do.

"But," they said, "there is no need to bring Jesus. It's too late."

Jesus stepped up to Jairus and said, "Don't be afraid. Just believe!"

At that moment, something about those words and the presence of Jesus kept Jairus from falling apart.

In spite of the messengers' advice, they traveled on together.

Room for Resurrection

As they entered the house, the commotion was loud and desperate.

Jairus' wife was weeping and wailing along with friends of the family. She was agonizing as only a mother can. Her friends cried with her.

Kindly, but firmly, Jesus demanded peace.

He said, "The child is not dead, but sleeping."

That brought a few mumbles, followed by some nervous scoffs and defiant snickers. "Who does this guy think he is?" they said. "Doesn't he know when to face reality?"

Jesus went into the little girl's room with Jairus and his wife and picked up the little girl's cold, pale, lifeless hand.

He said, "Little girl, get up!"

The girl woke up, just as she always did after having been asleep. She rose from her bed. Her parents hugged her and cried tears of joy.

"Get her something to eat" Jesus said.[68]

Parent Power

Parents can give children a chance to be with the champion in two ways.

First, invite Jesus into your child's bedroom.

Second, get them something nourishing to eat!

Welcome Jesus in through music. Invite Him in through scripture, pictures, inspirational posters, and books with spiritual value. Make sure the child has a good Bible her or she can understand.

Put out the worldly heroes, posters, and musical lyrics that bring only death and destruction.

Whether children are allowed to eat in their rooms or not, parents need to provide them spiritual food.

Resurrection power becomes available to any child when the presence of Jesus is invited into the bedroom. Encouraging a child to have a daily relationship with the Lord begins in their personal space. Children are then transformed. They get a new beginning. The blessings will take any child from death into new life.

Some parents will scoff at this advice as doing no good because their children resist. They are already gone. The damage is done. It's too late to stand up to the children. Their rooms were long ago turned over.

"That's not who they really are."

But every wise parent knows it's never too late.

Wise parents don't allow Jesus to be locked out of their child's room.

Parents who want to raise a champion will make room for resurrection power.

Demonic Daughter

Everywhere Jesus traveled, he was met with cries for help.

Even when he tried to enter a community secretly, he could not escape the needs of the children.

Once, Jesus entered a foreign territory where he thought no one would know Him. He intended to lay low for a while and rest. Although that was his plan, God interrupted with bigger ideas. Even on vacation, taking a break, whatever we are doing, children are worth interruptions.[69]

A loud and determined knock came to the door where Jesus was staying. A woman cried out to be let in. Her daughter had an evil spirit.

She yelled, "Have mercy on me, Lord! My daughter is suffering terribly from demon possession!"

Children's Crumbs

The whole neighborhood heard the yelling, and the woman was finally allowed to enter the house.

She rushed in and fell at Jesus' feet. She'd never seen Him, but she knew who He was. She could tell, just by looking, on which of the men the whole room centered.

The disciples urged Jesus to send her away. After all, she was loud and hysterical, and they could never get any rest with her desperate ranting. They could never keep their presence a secret.

Jesus looked at her quietly, calming her down.

Eventually, all in the house were silent, waiting to see what Jesus would do.

He tested her faith. He gave her a bit of a hard time. He did the same with his best friends, who urged Him to dismiss her. In front of all of them, He said to the woman, "It's not right to take the children's bread and toss it to the dogs".

The woman was not provoked or angry. She didn't have time to be angry, short, or smart. There was no time to lose sight of her only purpose. She did not argue with her daughter's only hope for healing. She responded in humility and love.

"Yes, Lord, but the dogs under the table eat the children's crumbs."

Mother Matters

It didn't matter to the mother what they thought.

The disciples considered her an outsider.

If Jesus had really thought she was beyond help, it would not have mattered. She would have still begged.

Her determination spoke volumes. She said, "Lord, help me! You feed your people all the time. What about me? Don't disqualify me on some technicality! Why can't I be on your team? Invisible, imaginary borders between our lands can't change my reality! I have feelings too, and I have a daughter. She needs help! I've heard you are helping so many people. What about my daughter? What about me?"

The woman's persistence was an obvious sign of faith, a refuse-to-give-up attitude!

"Call me what you want!" she continued. "If you consider me a beggar, I'll beg. If you consider me an outsider, I'll beg my way inside. If you consider me a dog, I'll gladly be a house dog and eat the crumbs falling from your table! I'll lick the floor to eat the life-giving bread you feed your disciples every day. It doesn't matter what you call me. It doesn't matter what your disciples think. It doesn't matter what anyone else thinks!"

There is only one thing that matters to a mother whose daughter is suffering.

Not religion, not social etiquette, not racial differences. Gender issues don't matter. Class distinction and wealth do not matter.

"My daughter is all that matters!"

What a great world we would live in if parents had that single supreme focus on their children! God is pleased when mothers make their children top priority.

And He acts!

Jesus answered, "Woman, your faith is great! Go home a champion! The demon has left your daughter!"

Second-Class Spirit

We will never know what was meant by the demon possession.

An evil spirit may consist of many bad things capable of taking complete control. The story doesn't tell what exactly caused the girl's suffering. The Scriptures do that by design because it doesn't really matter. We fill in the blanks. A long list of things can cause daughters to suffer: mood disorders, anxiety, depression, jealousy, drugs.

Each one is a demon to one degree or another.

Even though it's not clear what the demon was, there is one thing we can be sure of in this story.

An evil spirit makes our children second-class to other adult priorities.

God Is Good

Not everyone gets a chance with the Champion.

Overpowering evil can render a child helpless and unable to go to Jesus. There is no chance for the child to express faith.

Even with good, loving parents, by no choice of their own, some children find themselves in a distant land, removed from any relationship with Jesus.

Blessings are rare. Evil governs their lives, so they suffer.

Even then, a champion parent may encounter the Christ in an intercessory way.

To be a champion means to take up the cause of another, to support and defend. The word "champion" has much the same meaning as intercession—that is, pleading the case for another.

Champion parents call upon Jesus. When they encounter Christ, they put their priorities in the right place, with children at the top.

The faith of a determined parent who falls at the feet of the Christ, begging repeatedly, refusing to give up, can save a child who appears to have no hope.

When children cry, God hears. When parents cry, God cares.

God is honored when parents make their children top priority. It moves Him. He turns their lives around.

The forces of evil succumb to the powers of a good God.

Powerless People

A concerned exasperated father looked at his son.

It was hard to watch the boy being destroyed. In his eyes, the situation was almost hopeless. His son was possessed by an evil spirit.

The boy had a severe communication and medical disorder. He was deaf and mute. He suffered from convulsions. Sometimes he foamed at the mouth, ground his teeth, and then became stiff as a board. Near fire or water, he fell into seizures at the strangest most dangerous times. The boy constantly needed to be rescued.

He needed more than help. He needed healing.

There was only one person, only one who could give his son the chance he needed: the Champion himself!

A large crowd gathered around. They expected Jesus to arrive. The father got there early.

When he arrived, the waiting disciples were talking about how great they had become. They listed the amazing things they had done while encountering the Christ Champion. Since they had been traveling with Jesus, they were talking up their abilities.

"Yep," they said, "Jesus is great, and we are right there with Him."

They even argued publicly about who among them was the greatest of all. Perhaps one or two of them had actually healed someone in the name of Jesus! Obviously, being in the presence of all that power had gone to their heads!

With all the hype, the father could not wait. He asked the disciples to go ahead and heal his son, but in front of that great crowd, when the boy was brought near the disciples, nothing changed.

Nothing happened.

There was no power.

Small Seed

Jesus finally arrived.

The father explained that he had asked the disciples to heal his boy, but they couldn't. The situation remained critical. This was no small, easy request.
He said, "Jesus, if you can take pity on us. Help my boy and me."

Jesus took issue with the words. The father had one foot in the realm of faith. He had the other foot in disbelief.

"What do you mean, 'If you can'? Everything is possible for he who believes! Nothing is impossible for you. All it takes is a little faith; faith as small as a mustard seed."

The boy's father exclaimed, "I do believe! Help me overcome my disbelief!"

Then, as the boy was in the middle of being attacked by the evil one, Jesus commanded the evil spirit to come out of him. The boy convulsed violently and shrieked. Then, suddenly, he was still, so still and so calm he appeared to be dead.

Jesus took him by the hand, and the boy rose to his feet, clearly in his right mind, obviously changed and miraculously healed.

Prayer Power

The disciples asked Jesus, "Why couldn't we drive the demon out of the boy?"

He answered, "This kind can come out only through prayer!"

The story doesn't tell us where or when Jesus prayed. Perhaps He prayed very quickly as He sprang into action, seeing the crowd doubling in size. Perhaps Jesus always stayed "prayed up." We will never know. Details may be left out on purpose so we can focus on what we do know.

Evidently, the point is not when, where, or how we pray.

Jesus makes one thing clear: Praying for children is like the miraculous moving of a mountain. Praying for children is a key to doing the impossible in their lives.[70] Nothing is impossible in the lives of children who have praying parents.

Perfect faith is not a requirement. Big faith is not a necessity. A little genuine faith is what is needed.

Quality counts, not quantity.

No matter how difficult the situation in which our children and their caregivers find themselves, no matter how unbelievable it might be to think healing is possible, prayer and a little faith will win over doubt.

The power of Jesus will come forth.

Promoted and Praised

"Hey, kid," Jesus called. "Do me a favor! Stand here in the middle of this circle for a few minutes. I want to tell my friends how great you are! I want them to have a good look at greatness!"[71]

Imagine how that child felt, called out in a crowd, promoted and praised!

That's how Jesus treated kids.

All the grown-up VIPs were there. Very important people were hanging out.

We don't know whether the youngster belonged to one of the disciples or was simply playing near where they happened to be.

What made him so great?

Jesus didn't say, "Hey, guys, this kid made the honor roll! He's a gifted and talented young man!"

He didn't say, "Fellas, let me tell you about this girl. She is a great athlete!"

There were no accolades or ribbons on display from the county fair. None of the usual performance indicators were discussed. It appears that none of our common criteria mattered as Jesus evaluated the child's greatness, yet Jesus praised and promoted the child above all the disciples who were contemplating their own greatness.

There's only one thing we know this child did: he stood out in the crowd, as Jesus had asked.

That's it!

Women's Work

We don't know whether Jesus even knew this child.

The kid is never identified, but he stood front and center while Jesus launched one of His longer sermons. The title of the sermon was "Change! Become Like Little Children!"

Don't be confused by the term "little children."

Jesus wasn't excluding older children. He did not practice exclusion.

He was expanding the minds of his followers. He was inclusive.

"Don't overlook the very small!" He said.

In his day, adults often excluded the younger children. In their minds, little children had little to offer the world. The world could only wait until they grew up and were ready to work. Until then, little children were pretty much "women's work." The men had important things to do that did not involve little children.

The world hasn't changed its thinking much in two thousand years.

Performance or Person

The disciples argued among themselves.

They debated a question they hoped might someday be recorded in the history books.

Who among them was greatest?

Of course, they assumed Jesus was going down in history as the greatest, but who among His followers would be the greatest?

John thought he was best friends with Jesus. We wouldn't put it past Peter to say he had the greatest devotion. Matthew thought he kept the best records on Jesus and knew Him better than anyone else.

Somewhere along the way, they missed the point.

Our Heavenly Father's focus is not on the child's performance, nor is it on the disciples' abilities or bravery.

The Heavenly Father's focus is on the person!

Those who think they will be in heaven because of performance are subject to disqualification.

The disciples must have thought they could argue their way to heaven because, when Jesus walked up, they were still arguing.

Heaven's Humility

Jesus questioned the disciples.

What subject matter could require such attention and fervor?

They didn't want to tell Him exactly, so they posed it as a theological question, rather than a selfish one.

Who is the greatest in the kingdom of heaven?

Jesus gave them an answer that shook their world to its very foundation. He told them, "Change your attitude or you will never be there!"

Wow! Talk about a wake-up call!

Then Jesus called over a little child, just old enough to stand before a crowd, just old enough to respond to his request. He put the child, a kindergartener just graduating to the first grade, out in front of the group of arguing adults. He spoke a simple, yet stunning, truth: Great people aren't found in heaven. People who change are! Those who grow up are! Only children and those who are willing to become like children are found in God's Kingdom.

Those who value children the way Jesus does are the humble and accepting residents of heaven.

Heaven's Happiness

Jesus warned His best friends that every child has at least one angel watching over him or her.[72]

That angel always has access to the main throne room in heaven. That angel can meet face to face with the Heavenly Father at a moment's notice.

Heaven has commissioned the spiritual world to look out for the children. Heaven is a busy place!

Adults must tread carefully in the company of children. Those who lead children into sin and temptation will be held accountable in the highest possible terms. Jesus used the strongest warnings and words for all who look down on children. Instead, Jesus challenges us to look up to them![73]

If, like a lost sheep, only one little child wandered off, Jesus would search for him or her. Even if Jesus had to leave His busy schedule and important agenda, the Champion is not willing for one child to be lost.[74]

Children top all for Jesus! They rate! Nothing makes Him happier than children who come to Him.[75]

Jesus took the little boy in His arms and picked him up.[76] "Hey, kid!" he said, "thanks for your time! Thanks for being great. Thanks for showing us what we must become!"

Including Infants

Jesus cherished the children.

The disciples didn't get it. Jesus had a hard time getting through. They did not understand just how much he valued his time spent with children.

When Jesus urged His friends to become children, He couldn't have been including babies and lap children, could he? Surely Jesus could see that the wee ones were different.[77]

Okay, His friends weren't that dense. They got the earlier message that Jesus valued the kindergartner. They accepted the merit of kids who were starting school. They heard dozens of lectures that pointed out, "Our children are our future!"

But babies?

Then Jesus went a step farther in expanding the minds of his friends. In fact, He went all the way to including the infants.

Unlike the kindergartner, the babies could not be called over. They had to be brought to Jesus by caregivers: adults, parents, and grandparents.

Jesus said, "Let them come."

He held the babies and toddlers. He prayed for them and blessed them. He welcomed those who brought them.

Bothered with Babies

The disciples saw it as a waste of time.

Important things had to be done.

They were Jesus' bodyguards and protectors. His public schedule and travel plans, all interviews and appointments— everything was arranged through them. People would have to take a number and wait in line.

If Jesus was to be about changing the world, He shouldn't be so approachable. Everyone should have to wait their turn. Children and parents should not spontaneously, randomly come and go as they please. That's chaotic. Rules and order are needed. Priorities and strategic plans must be made to avoid interruptions, surprises, and curve balls.

From Children to Champions!

Jesus' friends fussed at the families who were bringing the babies and sent them away.

"Sorry, people," they said. "We know you've heard of Jesus and that word is getting around, but the Master has an extremely busy agenda. He already has places to go, people to see. He can't be bothered with these little ones!"

The families started to leave, but Jesus was indignant. He was angry with His friends' restrictive approach to matters important to the Heavenly Father.

He resented their attitudes.

He reminded the disciples what he had already told them: "Don't hold them back! Don't hinder them!"

"But Lord," Jesus' friends protested, "that was different before. These children are smaller than little kindergartners and first-graders! They can't even talk. They only babble!"

"Let them come. I like to be bothered with babies!

Toddlers are no trouble! Lap children are lovely!"

Kids' Kingdom

Then Jesus taught His best friends a basic principle to help them understand.

"The kingdom of heaven belongs to the kids!"

Wait a minute, now. Did we hear that right?

Didn't Jesus intend to say it another way? Didn't he mean to say, "The kids belong in the kingdom"?

That's what we think. That's the way we hear it every time. Adults are almost incapable of hearing it any other way. We think we need to reach the kids and teach the kids until finally, when they get into the Kingdom, we have done our job and have victory.

That's not what Jesus said.

He may have said it that way to the adults, "If you don't change to become like children, you can't enter the Kingdom."

But not for the kids!

The Kingdom belongs to them. They already have it. They have ownership. No membership applications necessary. No performance issues to qualify.

If you are a kid, you are heaven's corporate stockholder.

Motivational Minute

Before the families could get away, Jesus called them back.

One by one, he hugged the toddlers and held the babies.

He blessed them! The helpless! The dependent! Those who can give nothing in return!

It was the very best use of His time. It helped him get His priorities straight. It motivated Him for the road ahead. It made Him more effective for the task before Him.

What's that? Wait a minute. Did we mean to say it prepared Him for the cross?

Yes.

It was a messy, fussy, and bossy scene.

Parents apologized. Jesus laughed!

"Hey Jesus, you might want to wash Your hands and clean up a little," they said. "Some of those kids needed a fresh diaper. And you have a little drool running down your back where the babies spit up on you."

"It's okay!" Jesus said with a big smile. "My Heavenly Father told me that would happen. I was sent here especially for those who would spit on Me."

Greatest Gift

God loves children.

No matter what their age or circumstance, He wants to display His power in their lives.

Children are His true avengers and superheroes who defeat the enemies of God.[78]

The children we tend to think are less gifted are mighty in His eyes. God has a special place in His heart and a wonderful plan in mind even for children we think are handicapped or disadvantaged. No child is left behind. None is accidentally overlooked.

When passing out His favors, God equips each child with a unique, special, unexpected, magical, and supernatural gift.

By His wonderful grace, God gives children many chances:
- a chance to show faith,
- a chance to be healed,
- a chance to see,
- a chance to obey.

But for all His love and favors, none of it can happen without His greatest gift of all.

That's when God gives his child ... a chance to be with the Champion!

Christian parents, too, can give that greatest gift to children. They can bless their children in many ways, the same way parents did with Jesus!

After all, in the land of Is Real, a kid just needs a chance to be a champion!

Endnotes

Introduction
1. Psalm 8:2
2. I John 4:4

Chapter 1
3. Matthew 1:18
4. Matthew 13:56
5. Mark 6:3
6. I Corinthians 7
7. Hebrews 12:2, NLT. "We do this by keeping our eyes on Jesus, the champion who initiates and perfects our faith. Because of the joy awaiting him, he endured the cross…."
8. Hebrews 2:17-18, 4:15-16

Chapter 2
9. I Samuel 1:18
10. I Samuel 1:20
11. I Samuel 24, 28
12. I Samuel 2:1-10
13. I Samuel 2:18, 21
14. I John 4:4

15 I Samuel 2:17
16 I Samuel 2:29
17 I Samuel 2:26
18 I Samuel 3:18

Chapter 3

19 Genesis 25:22
20 Genesis 32:24
21 Genesis 32:25
22 Genesis 32:28
23 John 3:16

Chapter 4

24 II Samuel 9:7
25 Psalm 23
26 Jeremiah 29:11

Chapter 5

27 II Kings 5:3
28 II Kings 5:10
29 Luke 4:27

Chapter 6

30 John 18:2
31 Luke 22:38
32 John 18:6
33 Mark 14:51

Chapter 7

34 Exodus 1:22
35 Exodus 2:7
36 Ephesians 1:5

37 I Corinthians 10:13
38 James 4:7
39 Micah 6:4

Chapter 8

40 Deuteronomy 7:1
41 Numbers 13:32
42 Deuteronomy 3:11
43 I Samuel 17:4-7
44 I Samuel 17:28
45 Philippians 4:8
46 Ephesians 3:20
47 I Timothy 4:12
48 I Samuel 17:42-44

Chapter 9

49 Luke 15:11-32
50 Luke 15:13
51 Romans 3:23

Chapter 10

52 Esther 2:22
53 Esther 6:12
54 Esther 1:15
55 Matthew 10:32

Chapter 11

56 Genesis 37:2
57 Genesis 37:8
58 Genesis 39:2
59 Matthew 25:23
60 Genesis 39:21

61 Genesis 40:8
62 Genesis 41:16
63 Genesis 41:51,52
64 Genesis 45:8, 50:20

Chapter 12

65 I Kings 3:1-5
66 Hebrews 11:6
67 I Kings 3:7-9

Chapter 13

68 Matthew 9:18-26, Mark 5:21-43, Luke 8:40-56
69 Matthew 15:21-28, Mark 7;24-30
70 Matthew 17:14-21, Mark 9:14-29, Luke 9:37-43
71 Matthew 18:1-10, Mark 9:33-37, Luke 9:46-48
72 Matthew 18:10
73 Matthew 18:10
74 Matthew 18:14
75 Matthew 18:13
76 Mark 9:36
77 Matthew 19:3-15, Mark 10:13-16, Luke 18:15-17
78 Psalm 8:2

For more study:
Child Character Champion Checklist

Child Champion Identity _____

List the adversity, problems, or needs encountered.

Describe the child's solutions or actions in response.

What did the child or parents do to help the child?

How did God transform the child into a champion?

CPSIA information can be obtained at www.ICGtesting.com
Printed in the USA
LVOW13s1808240813

349379LV00001B/6/P

9 781449 770679